P.I.G.G.Y. Plan-It

Prudent Investors Get Going Young

Nancy Lottridge Anderson, Ph.D., CFA
Ryder Taff, CFA, CIPM
Susan E. McAdory, MBA

For sweet Ken and Retta, who make every day an adventure

—Nancy

For the P.I.G.G.Y.s

—Ryder

For Dr. Robert T. McAdory, Jr. and Pamela Pape, who put up with me
—Susan

Copyright © New Perspectives, Inc., 2018
All rights reserved

PIGGY Plan-It® is a trademark of New Perspectives, Inc.
Prudent Investors Get Going Young® is a trademark of New Perspectives, Inc.

Cover Art and Illustrations by Justin Ransburg

For more information, contact New Perspectives, Inc., 303 Highland Park
Cove, Suite B, Ridgeland, MS 39157
www.newper.com

P.I.G.G.Y. Plan-It: Prudent Investors Get Going Young / Nancy Lottridge
Anderson, Ph.D., CFA, Ryder Taff, CFA, CIPM, Susan E. McAdory, MBA
ISBN-13: 978-1-984-23364-6
ISBN-10: 1-98-423364-5

10 9 8 7 6 5 4 3 2 1

Printed in the United States of America.

The material contained in this book is not investment advice. Consult a
professional for advice on investment decisions.

CONTENTS

Introduction

Who Are You and Why Should I Listen to You?

These are excellent questions to ask anyone offering you financial advice. If everyone asked an advisor this right off the bat, there'd probably be a lot less regret further on down the line. If you take away one piece of advice from us, let it be to thoroughly check the credentials of a financial advisor.

P.I.G.G.Y. (Prudent Investors Get Going Young) Plan-It is an idea we came up with a few years ago. We wanted to find a way to educate our friends about personal finance without boring them to death. Surprisingly, not everyone is that interested in the topic. Unless you major in Finance or happen to have a keen interest in the stock market, it's unlikely that you have a solid grasp on investing.

That's where we come in. Our aim is to bring you up to speed and to help you navigate your finances.

Our first goal will be to motivate you to just get started. Know that we've been right where you are, green behind the ears with little income and no investments. Next, we provide you with sound, practical information about all aspects of your financial life. We'll make it easy to digest, instead of filling you full of technical jargon. After all, we want you to read this book and actually take action. And although this is a subject you shouldn't take lightly, we'll try to keep the subject fairly light.

We all work at New Perspectives, Inc., an independent, fee-only financial advisory firm located in Ridgeland, Mississippi. Mississippi has the lowest median household income in the country, and any Mississippian who has stuck around the state and has a little to show for it has learned a few things about money management.

Nancy started New Perspectives in 1993 and brought Ryder on board in 2011. A few years later, Nancy hired one of her M.B.A. students, Susan. Although the book reads as being told from a collective "we," most of the advice comes from Nancy and Ryder. Between the three of us, we have about 40 years of experience in the field. Combine that with a set of respected credentials and a determination to always put our clients first, and you have a trio with some worthwhile things to say.

Since Nancy has the most years of experience in the field, she introduces herself more personally on the next two pages.

We hope you find this book useful and that it inspires you to become a prudent investor early in life. After all, Prudent Investors Get Going Young! So, get to it, P.I.G.G.Y.

Meet Nancy:

Thirty-two seems like ages ago. Where did the time go?

That's the thing about life. You're just busy "doing it," and it's just flying by. At fifty-nine, I feel the sense of urgency. I'm counting the number of possible years left—the number of summers, anniversaries, holidays—and I know I better get going.

At thirty-two, urgency is not natural. You think "this," whatever "this" is, will last forever. You have all the time in the world. In fact, things seem to be moving too slowly. And you put off doing some very important things, like managing your money and saving for retirement, because: What's the hurry?

At thirty-two, time is on your side. In a few short decades, time will bear down on you to the point that you won't be able to breathe! And you'll wonder: Where did the time go?

When I was thirty-two, my first husband died of cancer, and I was left with a child to raise on my own. I had the gifts of some life insurance, a good mind and a dogged determination to give my daughter a good life.

By happenstance, I found myself working for a financial advisor when we received Keith's terminal diagnosis. Thankfully, I learned the value of saving and living reasonably from my parents, but I never learned about investing. Now, I was thrown into the middle of this world, and I figured out that I love business! And I learned that the world of investing allows me to study all kinds of businesses. What fun!

I also realized this world is full of men. Yet, more and more women needed help navigating the financial world—women who never married, women who were divorced, and women like me who found themselves widowed. So I watched and learned from the financial advisor who was my employer, applied my personal experience to the mix, and headed back to school for my M.B.A. all in an effort to step up as a financial advisor in my own right. But it was not to be, at least not there.

3

My boss was old school, parading as a liberal, forward-thinking man. When it came down to it, he said, "I just don't think I can have a woman as an equal partner." Life happened again and forced me to step out on my own. At the time, it was anything BUT a sure thing. Today, I can say that it was the best thing that happened to me.

I found my voice and my platform, speaking to all about the importance of wise money management. For over twenty-five years, I have worked with individuals and small businesses to help them weather financial storms and prepare for long-term security. I am passionate about educating people about the world of finance, and I am willing to talk to anyone who will listen. I know that whatever your age, getting control of your money is an urgent matter.

Along the way, I finished that M.B.A. and received my designation as a Chartered Financial Analyst. Further, I completed my Ph.D. in Business Administration with a concentration in Finance. Life handed me experience, but I pursued knowledge. I understood the value of the combination.

Today, I continue to work with clients one-on-one to develop financial plans and help with financial troubles. I manage portfolios on an ongoing basis to assist people who are preparing for retirement and those who are already retired and living out of that precious portfolio. Several years ago, I added classroom duties to my list. That allows me to educate college students about finance and the world of investing. I try to convey a sense of urgency to those 20-somethings.

When it comes to my favorite topic, I use every media available. I talk to groups. I write articles. I am a host on a call-in radio show about finance called "Money Talks," and I appear regularly on a local television show to convey financial tips.

Because time is flying by! So, whether you are twenty, thirty, or getting up there like me, there is no time like the present to get your financial house in order. Making the time to take care of this one area of your life will give you the freedom to make life-changing choices. Hurry! This is urgent!

Don't suffer fools. Figure out who is worth listening to.

An Intro to the Field

Interestingly, the financial advisor profession is one of a handful of careers that doesn't yet have required professional oversight. Anyone can be a financial advisor as long as you can pass an examination. This means that it's important for you to know what you're looking for in an advisor.

A few qualifications to look for:

- How many years of industry experience does the advisor have?

- Does the advisor have a college degree from a reputable institute?

- What certifications does the advisor hold?

- Does the advisor have any violations?

You value your money and your time, and you don't want to spend too much of either on a relationship you're not comfortable with. A financial advisor is a position of trust—not only the trust not to make off with your funds in the night, but also the confidence that you can tell this person both your dreams and your fears. Your advisor should work towards positioning you financially so that you can focus more on achieving your goals and waste less time with worry.

Through the course of this relationship, your life will change. You may start a family or a business. You may decide you need a year to explore. You may have large medical expenses or need to take care of your parents as they age. Although you may not be able to map exactly how your life will unfold, you can develop a plan that anticipates the unexpected. It makes sense to put in the time necessary on the front end to find the advisor who is the right fit for you.

While you should ask questions about how the advisor would handle specific concerns of yours or issues unique to your situation, there are some general questions that you *must* have answered.

How Does the Advisor Get Paid?

This is the single most important question. The answer to this question gives you clues to the advisor's philosophy and approach. It also tells you something about the legal restraints under which she operates. (More about that under the section on credentials!)

No matter how good someone is at managing your money or providing advice, if someone other than you is paying the advisor, there is an opportunity for a conflict of interest. Payment for services can either come as commissions, fees or both. Advisors working on commission get paid based on a product they sell you. This motivates them to sell you more of the product and to sell you more of a product that has a higher commission. Advisors who accept commissions from third parties may have a conflict of interest that needs to be disclosed to you.

While there's nothing wrong with using a commission broker, the problem is that most people don't read the fine print. They don't know that buying mutual fund A may cost them more than buying mutual fund B. While brokers are required to disclose this information, they are not required to shout it! The truth is that most clients walk away from those transactions blissfully ignorant—until their statements arrive.

A fee-only advisor is paid only through fees for service to clients. The fees can take many shapes—hourly work, fees for specific actions or fees for assets under management—but they are paid by the client. Ask how the advisor's fee structure incentivizes her to work for you.

In the middle of commission brokers and fee-only advisors, there are "fee-based" advisors who may earn some combination of a fee and a commission.

If YOU are the only one paying your advisor, it's clear the advisor is working for YOU. If someone or some company is padding the advisor's bank account, the result is not as clear. The difference is one between an advisor and a salesperson. Everyone works for money – make sure they are working for YOUR money!

Are They Certified? What Are Their Credentials?

Next—and this applies to any advice you're seeking—you're going to want to figure out whether or not you should be listening to this person. Does this person know what they're talking about? We've all heard stories of people being conned by charming chameleons claiming to be experts in a field (particularly in the field of finance). Because the industry is so fractured and certifications are not standard, the guy selling you stocks today could be the guy selling you a used car last week!

What are the areas of finance? AKA—why is my car insurance guy trying to get me to open an IRA?

First, a little history. Back in 1929, the stock market crashed, and The Great Depression hung over the decade of the 1930s. It was terrible!

Investors jumped out of windows. Bread lines cropped up everywhere. Banks closed their doors. Sounds a little like the Financial Crisis of 2008? Hmmm...

In 1932, Congress passed the Glass Steagall Act. One of the provisions of this new law was to build walls in between different types of financial institutions. Banks could only do deposits and lending. Insurance companies could only offer insurance products. And brokers could only sell stocks, bonds and mutual funds. The idea was to keep each one in its respective lane to avoid a system-wide crash again. And it worked!

That is, it worked until 1999, when Glass Steagall was repealed with the signing of the Gramm Leach Bliley Act. We guess sixty years is enough for anyone (doesn't anyone stay together anymore?), and suddenly, all bets were off. Everybody could do EVERYTHING. Bankers met you at the door pushing life insurance. Your property insurance guy tried to sign you up for a mortgage. And the stockbrokers got in everybody's business. Confusion reigned.

After all, those "experts" in each field are now supposed experts in EVERY area of finance. How did they gain the knowledge and experience?

The credentials for an insurance agent are focused on insurance products. Tests that stockbrokers take to sell securities are focused on securities. And bankers go to banking school. Each area has its own exams and certifications. Know that not all are equal. Ask your advisor for his or her certifications. Find out who awards these certifications and what they mean. Find out if your advisor really does possess that particular credential. Go online or call the organization that makes the award. Don't assume a bunch of letters behind someone's name means something.

Brokers and insurance agents must take "Series" exams in order to sell investment products. These exams are numbered, and the number determines what products they can sell and what role they can play.

Sometimes, an advisor will push a particular product just because of the limitations under the Series exams. Ask for which exams they have passed. The National Association of Securities Dealers (NASD) tracks licensing and complaints on agents through the FINRA system. You should be able to look up an advisor's record. One word of caution: even one complaint is rare. Most people simply walk away without registering a formal complaint, so having even one complaint on file is concerning. Two is a raging fire!

States regulate small and medium-sized (around up to $100 million assets under management) registered investment advisers (RIAs). RIAs operate under different guidelines than commission brokers and insurance agents. Regardless, you should find them in the FINRA system.

Each state has its own requirements for RIAs. In Mississippi, an RIA must either hold the CFA (Chartered Financial Analyst) designation or must past certain Series exams in order to dole out advice. Larger RIAs will be regulated by the Securities and Exchange Commission (SEC).

Want to track down the records on your advisor? (You do.)

- Search for the advisor on FINRA: https://brokercheck.finra.org/,

- through the SEC: https://www.sec.gov/reportspubs/investor-publications/investor-brokershtm.html,

- or contact your state's Secretary of State's office.

The most important thing you need to do is to make sure your advisor is legitimate and has been conducting herself appropriately.

What about other designations? Well, there are many! A few that are well-known and well-respected include CFA and CFP. Nancy and Ryder hold the CFA (Chartered Financial Analyst) designation. You can visit the CFA Institute's website at www.cfainstitute.org to find out more about this credential and to check them out. This designation is heavy on portfolio management, quantitative techniques and ethics.

CFP stands for Certified Financial Planner. The focus on this course of study is comprehensive personal finance. Check this out at www.cfp.net. Both the CFA and the CFP designations require a college degree, an exam (three exams for the CFA designation, one for the CFP), years of experience and a commitment to abide by a list of ethical tenants.

Other designations are out there. And, again, what you need to do first is to find out if the person you're thinking about taking advice from has REALLY earned those letters. That's easy enough to do. We have the Internet. Don't just take someone's word for it. Next, research the quality of the organization making the award. How rigorous are the qualifications for the designation?

Who Makes Portfolio Decisions and How?

If you ever have any deeper questions about why your investment recommendations are what they are, you want to speak to the person who actually makes these decisions. Your advisor may outsource management or even advice to another company or to a computer program. None of this is inherently bad, but it is good to know where the decisions are being made and what the limitations are.

Many advisors are using third-party managers. This means the advisor signs you up, chooses a model portfolio and then allows someone else to trade on the account per the pre-assigned model. Ask about the performance record of a third-party advisor. Make sure the trading won't cost you in fees or taxes.

If your advisor does it all themselves, ask about performance. You can even ask for referrals. Most importantly, make sure there is a separate, recognized CUSTODIAN who handles the money and securities. That would be a company such as TD Ameritrade, Schwab, Wells Fargo, etc. You don't want to get "Madoffed"* by someone who takes your money and then invents a phony portfolio on paper. There should be independent handling of money and securities as well as independent reporting to verify what your advisor is providing to you.

*"Madoffed" refers to the infamous Bernie Madoff who scammed his clientele (many very wealthy and famous people) by pocketing their money after they entrusted him to invest their funds.

A couple of lessons to learn from this:

- Verify the statements your advisor gives you with those produced by a third party (the custodian). Do they match? You're going to want to be able to check for yourself. Do NOT blindly trust your advisor.

- When writing checks or transferring funds to be invested by your advisor, be sure you're putting this with the custodian, not with your advisor. Do NOT make out a check in your advisor's name or in the name of your advisor's company (e.g.: Mom and Pop, LLC). If the third party custodian is TD Ameritrade, for example, then that is the custodian of your account, and it is to TD Ameritrade that you are transferring your funds.

What is the Advisor's Work History and Education?

Hopefully, you have checked out your prospective advisor on FINRA's BrokerCheck and have maybe conducted a Google or LinkedIn search, but hear it from the advisor, too. Ask about education, experience and credentials. While these don't mean everything, it is important that your advisor have a broad base of knowledge to deal with any questions that you may have. Many industry certifications require continuing education so that their members stay up to date with changes in that professional world.

Read the advisor's Form ADV. This form is filed with the advisor's regulators and lists all education, credentials and relevant industry experience. It's not very exciting, but it can be quite informative. In addition to listing the advisor's history, the Form ADV will also tell you which services are offered by the advisor, how the advisor charges fees, what types of clients the advisor work with and more.

How Are You Protected from the Advisor?

Don't be afraid to ask: What happens if you try to scam me? Third party custodians, watchful regulators and open communication go a long way towards preventing fraud. An advisor should understand the deep fear of losing everything to fraud and be able to demonstrate how you are protected. The ability to withdraw your money without penalty or to transfer your accounts to another advisor are powerful tools for keeping your advisor in check. Make sure that you retain full ownership of your assets at all times.

The flip side of this question is to find out if your advisor is a fiduciary. A fiduciary is someone who has an obligation to put your interests first. When making decisions, a fiduciary does not consider any personal benefit she may receive from the outcome. This is generally the highest standard of advisors.

Fiduciary is a legal term. We usually put the word "duty" with it: fiduciary duty. This means you have an obligation to act in someone else's best interest—to not put yourself first. We usually hear this "prudent man rule"—you must act as a prudent man, using reason, care and skill. Understand that prudence is in the eye of the beholder, so it's really quite subjective. But, it's this idea that I'm not going to act in MY best interest; I'm going to act in the best interest of the person I'm working for (my client/the person I'm serving).

In finance, the question is: Who is a fiduciary? We're having a big battle about this right now, because we have a broad range of people who work in the area of finance ranging from insurance salesmen to commission brokers to investment advisors. An investment advisor—someone who is a Registered Investment Adviser (RIA)—we are—under the State of

Mississippi or under the Securities and Exchange Commission (SEC), is under the legal obligation to act as a fiduciary (to act in the client's best interest). It makes sense that the advisor would be under this obligation.

But, who is not a fiduciary? Actually, commission brokers. They have a lower standard related to suitability. Suitability means you are selecting investments that are suitable based on that client's particular needs and goals. Suitability means to make selections that are appropriate; fiduciary means that not only must selections be appropriate, they must also be the best selections. Fiduciary is a higher standard. These are the standards under which you would sue if you had a complaint. Suitability allows an advisor to point you to products that pay them more. That wouldn't fly with the fiduciary.

There is a move under way to change this, and the commission broker industry is kind of fighting this. As of 2017, any commission brokers offering advice on retirement accounts must also adhere to the fiduciary standard. However, accounts funded before the rule took effect in June of 2017 may be grandfathered in under the old suitability standard, so be careful not to assume that the account is suddenly operating under the higher standard. And for non-retirement accounts, the old suitability standard is still in play.

We are on the side of, well, why not adhere to the higher standard? You should be doing this anyway. But, it's buyer beware! Understand what the word "fiduciary" means and that it's okay for you to ask when you talk to someone about your finances: Are you a fiduciary?

Conflicts of Interest

A fiduciary is required to make all decisions in your best interest. Generally, this means avoiding conflicts of interest, but motivations are tricky things, and conflicts can be found just about anywhere.

At New Perspectives, we have been fiduciaries from the get-go. Two of us (Nancy and Ryder) are CFA charterholders and are proud of the fact that we hold ourselves to such a high standard. From what we have seen from clients that come to us, acting in a client's best interest not only makes sense, but can be very profitable for the clients themselves. When past advisors have not acted in clients' best interests, their accounts have suffered.

We preach a no-conflict relationship to our clients every time we see them. A fiduciary relationship is clearly spelled out in our contract. We don't just call ourselves fiduciaries, we are fiduciaries. To think that we might have substantial conflicts doesn't appear to align with what we say! But, conflicts of interest are still possible. We've thought through a few examples.

To start, we are fee-only advisors. Literally, our only source of income comes from clients paying us for advice. For clients that pay us for hourly advice, we strive to make sure we don't spend unnecessary time on a task or bill them for doing something that is not strictly relevant to the advice we are giving them. For clients who pay us an ongoing fee to manage accounts, our motivation is clearly to keep managing their money and to manage more of it! Here are how some conflicts might arise:

- We are motivated to manage as much of a client's money as possible. If a client has a lot of cash or outside investments, we would want to manage that as well. To mitigate this, we typically recommend that people leave cash in a bank they are comfortable doing business with and give an honest assessment of whether or not we think their assets would be better managed under our umbrella. If the assets would be better left alone, we make it clear to the client what the differences would be. While a conflict may exist here, we are aware of it and still make decisions in the best interest of the client.

- While we do not have any performance-related fees on accounts, we are still motivated for the accounts to grow. We know, however, that short term performance will likely increase long term risks in a client's portfolio. Our motivation is to prudently serve a client over time, not just for another quarter. Our portfolio decisions are still made with the client and current market conditions in mind.

- It is often thought that we prefer only large accounts and will therefore pay less attention to smaller accounts. While a conflict may exist where we prefer to service a larger account, the setup of our office and the technology available to us makes this concern practically nonexistent. We can trade in a small account just as easily as in a large account, and the other financial advice needs of one average human are the same regardless of account size. While we do service accounts of all different sizes for people of all different needs, all of our clients get the best service we can offer.

- We may have a motivation to post higher numbers at the end of a quarter (when we bill), but that is not technically possible with us. Our assets are held at a third party, and any report we make can be verified with them. Additionally, our clients are invested in publicly traded securities with easily verifiable values. If we boosted those numbers, it would be worse than a conflict; it would be fraud. In that vein, we have a section of our website dedicated to the ways that clients are protected from possible conflicts, malfeasance or incompetence.

In light of these potential conflicts, we are still comfortable telling clients that we will work in their best interests. We do see conflicts arise during decision-making, but we will always act in a client's best interest. We truly believe that we achieve our long term best interest by serving our clients' best interests every day.

What Does the Relationship Look Like to the Advisor?

Make sure you are on the same page here. You approach an advisor because you have specific current needs and unknown future needs. Make sure that they are aware of what you will need from them, as well as how often and proactively you would like them to communicate with you.

Selecting a financial advisor is selecting someone for your personal Board of Directors. You need to trust this person's ability, integrity and dedication to the task. You have a right to know how your advisor works, gets paid and makes decisions. Hopefully, this will be a long and fruitful relationship, and it will take effort on both sides to maintain it.

Don't suffer fools. Figure out who is worth listening to.

Your Two To-Do Lists:

Before Meeting an Advisor:

- Check them out online. Look at the company's website and/or a resume on LinkedIn.

- If they list any letters behind their names (CFA, CFP, etc.), verify with the organization that they have actually earned this designation and are keeping it current.

- Look the advisor up on FINRA's BrokerCheck. Check to see which exams they have passed and what products or services the exams allow them to advise you on. While you're here, definitely look to see if they have any complaints filed against them!

- If you can, try to find a way to get a feel for the advisor's personality. You're going to want someone you are comfortable building a relationship with over the long term. Have they written any articles, columns, books, blogposts you can read? Maybe they have a radio show or a podcast you can catch a few episodes of to get an idea of the kind of advice they give. If you're active on social media, then check out the advisor's company pages. Is the material useful? Is it updated regularly?

- Likewise, you may want to be sure you can work with someone who communicates with you in a variety of ways. Are they easy to reach by phone? Do they promptly return calls? Do they respond quickly to emails? Is it easy to schedule a face-to-face meeting with them? If you're an out of town client, is the advisor able to do remote meetings?

During Your Meeting with an Advisor:

- Ask about the advisor's background:

    o Degree

    o Certifications

    o Experience.

- Ask how the advisor is paid and who all pays them.

- Ask if the advisor is a fiduciary.

- Ask who makes the investment decisions in the firm.

- Ask about the advisor's investment philosophy.

- Ask what will happen to you if something happens to the advisor. Is there someone else in the firm who will take over?

- Ask who custodies the accounts.

- Ask for a copy of the ADV and READ it. You don't need to do this while you're in the meeting, but you should read it over on your own time.

- Don't feel pressured to sign on with an advisor during the initial meeting. This is a serious decision, and you need to make it with confidence.

Don't suffer fools. Figure out who is worth listening to.

Advice that has Stood the Test of Time:

Nancy's Column from 1997: "Avoiding the Practices of a Greedy Broker"

Do you remember that old movie *Network*? About the only thing I remember is that the main character, a TV newscaster, gets fed up one night on the air. He starts screaming, "I'm mad as hell, and I'm not going to take it anymore." He works his viewers into a frenzy, encouraging them to repeat after him. Soon, people all over the country are leaning out their windows and screaming into the streets: "I'm mad as hell, and I'm not going to take it anymore!"

What's making me so mad? I'm mad at the people in my business who sully my reputation with their questionable and, sometimes, unethical practices. I'm mad about the people, older ones in particular, who are being led down the primrose path by greedy brokers and advisors.

And I'm mad at the people who base their selection of an advisor on the subjective, "But he seemed like such a nice man." I'd be nice too if you were lining my pockets! It's not always easy to tell if you're getting good advice, but there are some red flags.

Portfolios Full of Limited Partnerships and Unit Investment Trusts

While these MAY be appropriate for some clients in small doses, they are not good for the entire portfolio or even the bulk of it. Both securities are fairly illiquid. You can't convert them to cash easily, at least not without a sizable loss. Typically, you put money in these. They pay an income, and you have to wait for all properties to dissolve or all securities to mature before you can get your principal back.

While the income part may seem enticing to older people, consider the need to tap into principal should an emergency health situation occur. You'll be stuck with an investment you can't get your hands on. And

19

depending on the underlying securities, you may be getting into something fairly risky.

I don't use or recommend either of these investments. There are too many alternatives with greater flexibility and less risk. But I do know why I see them in client accounts. They are high commission payers, so beware.

Little Old Ladies with Annuities and Annuities within IRAs

Annuities were designed to avoid taxes. They are good vehicles for people in high tax brackets who are still trying to sock away money for retirement but have used up their IRA or retirement contributions for the year.

Most little old ladies don't have a tax problem. And they're not interested in retirement funds. They are already there! Since most annuities have high expenses and surrender charges lasting anywhere from six to nine years, these are quite unsuitable for your grandmother (or your mother). There are other investments out there that will give them safe, solid returns with the flexibility they need at this age.

And, NEVER, EVER use an annuity for your IRA. An IRA, by Congressional order, is tax-deferred already. Using an annuity for an IRA is like a bald man buying a blow dryer. It's an accessory he doesn't need. So, why pay extra for something you won't use?

And why am I seeing people with annuities who don't need them or shouldn't be in them? Well, they are, typically, high commission payers. Hmm... I think I said that before. Fixed annuities are about the only investment-type product that many insurance people are licensed to sell. Buyer beware!

High Turnover Rates in Portfolios

This means you are constantly buying and selling within the account. For many investments, the buy and hold strategy is the best. Too much turnover simply costs you in transaction costs and commissions. Make sure the changes you make in your portfolio put you in a better position.

When this practice gets out of hand, it's illegal and it's called churning. I recently saw a small account with 10 funds in it. The size of the account warranted three at most. In less than a year's time, all 10 funds were sold and switched to 10 other funds of the same type. The broker got a commission when the first 10 were purchased and another commission when the second 10 were bought. Because the account was spread over 10 investments, it was hard for the client to detect the commission deductions.

Which leads me to my final point. Most abuses occur because somebody is getting greedy. The most important question you can ask when you hire a broker or advisor is, "How do you make your money?" If you deal with a commission person, know the commission schedules of all recommended investments before making a decision. Check your statements for other expenses. Whether you choose a fee-only person or a commission person, the key is full disclosure.

Now, everybody go to your windows, stick your head out, and yell, "I'm mad as (a. hell, b. heck, c. a wet hen) and I'm not going to take it anymore!"

As a Wise P.I.G.G.Y. Once Said:

- Be wary of limited partnerships and unit investment trusts.

- Don't use IRA/retirement money to buy an annuity.

- Be cautious when it comes to annuities. They're inflexible and expensive.

- Beware of advisors who always want to make changes in your account.

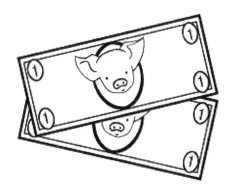

Align your values with your spending.

Goals

You know what a goal is. It's something you want but don't have yet.

A good goal brings you closer to happiness—or joy. Call it what you want. You're motivated to make yourself happy. How do you make yourself happy? Well, that's a complicated question, but, to start with, it's a good idea to find out what's most important to you.

What Are Your Values?

Safety. Financial Security. Family. Health. Travel. Community. Music. Animals. Justice. Food. TV. Sleep. Sanity.

We didn't list money. We don't think money is a value. Money has a value (obviously), but what we mean is that money is a way to obtain whatever it is that you value. Money isn't the end goal, but it's often the means to that goal.

Once you've figured out what your values are and which are most important to you, you can decide whether money is a tool you need to use to uphold those values. It's difficult to find a value that isn't greatly helped by money, but for those of us on a limited budget, we aren't going to be able to uphold all of our values with money.

If a value is important to you, but you don't see a place in your limited budget for it, you can spend another thing that's right up there with money on it: time. If you value a fine dining experience but can't afford to eat out, learn to cook your own five star meals. If you value Earth's creatures but can't afford a pet or a monthly donation to the Sierra Club, put in some time at your local animal shelter or volunteer at the zoo. Money doesn't need to be the only tool you use to uphold your values.

How Do You Figure Out What You're Currently Valuing?

If you want to figure out whether or not your current spending habits line up with your values and will help you reach your goals, take a look at where your money has been going for the last month. Unless you're shelling out cash for everything, you should be able to pull up your bank or credit card transactions online. Export them into a spreadsheet and categorize them (or feel free to do it by hand).

Once you see just where your money is going each month, it's easier to identify where you can make a change. If you realize you're throwing a lot of money away eating out at restaurants, sit down and write up a meal plan for the week. Stock your fridge and pantry with only what it takes to make those meals a reality, then compare. Were you spending more eating out or eating in?

This isn't to say you should always scrimp on dining. Maybe you're someone who values the dining experience and tasting new foods. Look elsewhere in your transaction history and see where you can cut your expenses.

Now that you have an idea of where you can cut costs and how much you will need and want to spend on certain areas of your life, build a budget. This isn't as tedious as it sounds. You've already identified what you're going to have to and *want* to spend your money on. Now, put these monthly amounts in your spreadsheet/worksheet.

Why Have Goals?

Goals simply make your life easier. Once you know where your values lie, you just have to decide what you want and how to get there. Once you figure that out, all you need to do is stick to the plan. After a while, look back at your goals. Check how you're coming along in your plan and adjust accordingly.

Examples

Your goals don't all have identical time frames. Some of your goals are very short-term. Some are recurring. Some don't have a definite date. As examples, we'll share a couple of our values and the goals we've set to fulfill them.

Short-Term Recurring Goal

VALUE: Susan likes to travel. She particularly likes mountains. She wants to take at least one big trip a year.

GOAL: She needs to save $3,000. Once she has this saved, she knows she can take the trip. This is a yearly goal.

PLAN: Set up an automatic transfer of $125 from her checking account to her savings account each time Susan gets paid. She gets paid twice a month, so after 12 months, she should have enough saved to take one big trip.

Long-Term Goal

VALUE: Susan wants to stop working (retire) one day. She wants the ability to spend the bulk of her time doing anything besides punching the proverbial clock.

GOAL: She needs to contribute to retirement accounts.

PLAN: Consider when she might see herself stepping away from work. Then, learn about retirement benefits offered by the company she works for. Participate in the program. Get advice on how much to set aside, what types of accounts to open and how to invest the funds.

By categorizing goals as short-term, medium-term or long-term, you'll get an idea of how to appropriately fund the goal. You'll match the term of the goal to the term of the investment. Short-term goals should be matched to short-term savings—money market accounts, short-term certificates of deposit. Long-term goals will be matched to long-term investments—stocks and bonds.

As a Wise
P.I.G.G.Y.
Once Said:

We've all heard the saying about what's paving the road to hell, but what about the road to paradise? How do you get to the good place?

Yes, life is going to throw us all curveballs. We will be blessed with both fortune and misfortune, success and failure. We will not end up exactly where we thought we'd be in precisely the manner we thought we'd get there. That being said, here are a few ways to help you navigate some of the hurdles:

- Know your values.

- Make a plan. (It can be loose and flexible.)

- Learn whom to trust for advice. You're going to want someone to turn to if plans change or if you get off track.

- Be open to change. Look at the unknown as an opportunity.

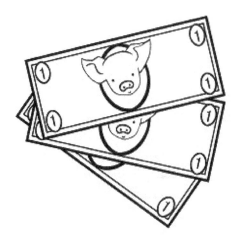

Build yourself a safety net.

A Brief History of Savings

When we look back at our savings habits, we see two different stories. From 1949 to 1984, our savings rates averaged 11.1% per year, and in none of those years did we save per household less than 9%. After 1984, we see a different story. Since then, we have never saved over 9%. Shockingly, in 2005, our average savings rate was only 2.6%! In the summer of 2008, before the Financial Crisis, we were at nearly zero on our savings rate. In 2009, we bumped back up to 6.1%, because that's what happens when we get scared. We're nervous about our jobs; we're concerned about the economy, and suddenly we start saving more.

Some of the change in our savings rate has to do with available government programs. Social Security and Medicare meant families could save less because their paychecks were already being drafted to cover some of those expenses through a government program. Certainly, we usually see higher savings rates in countries without any safety net program. The average savings rate in China is around 25%, but they are developing their own government programs so that 25% savings rate could change.

But something else has happened. We have easier access to credit and can use this to fall back on in a pinch. We can always pull out the card, right? Credit limits have climbed, allowing us to forget about saving all together. The result is that we've become a society operating under "gotta have it right now" versus "gotta save for it." The average savings rate currently is less than 5%. Now, that's sort of a good news/bad news situation, because when we save less, we're feeling more confident with the economy. But, of course, we have great concerns as financial advisors that we're not saving enough.

The question is: How much do you need to save?

When it comes to your retirement, we know based on research you need to save 16.6% every year for 30 years in order to replace your income in retirement. We also, in the meantime, have emergencies. We tell people to try to save 3 to 6 months' income to have in an emergency cash account (an emergency fund). That's pretty hard to do, but that amount of money will keep you out of the credit card ditch.

Emergency Fund

What goes in an emergency fund? Money. Cash. The thing is, we don't know what an emergency will look like so it's important that your emergency fund can cover all sorts of weird situations. Cash is king, as they say, and barring the end of the world, cash should still be good in your local jurisdiction. It may still even be good after the end of the world if nobody is quite sure what else to do.

Where do you put this cash? Let's think about what an emergency might look like. A fire. A devastating robbery. An accident whilst hiking in the Himalayas. You want cash, but don't just leave it in your wallet, under your mattress or in a jar underneath a tree. If it were under a tree that only you knew where to find, it would be rather difficult to pay a hospital bill in

Nepal. Can you imagine trying to explain to the billing department how you were planning on satisfying the bill? Even more nightmarish is if you were hiking without a permit—that $11,000 fine would not be satisfied by the laughter you would evoke from the friendly park rangers.

Put the cash in a bank account. We generally advise having an online savings account that is reasonably out of reach, sight and mind. You can probably find one that doesn't charge fees as long as you maintain a certain balance. Set it up so that you can transfer money back and forth from your checking account and go ahead and set up automated deposits into the account until you have built up a reliable reserve.

We recommend online bank accounts for a few reasons. You can typically get lower fees and a better interest rate online. This also means your money will be accessible wherever you are. And if this account is separate from your other banking activity, then the account is kept out of sight and out of mind—exactly where an emergency account should be. (You don't want to be tempted to dip into it without good cause.)

How much do you need to put in an emergency fund? This is the trick. Start with $1,000. Why? It's a nice number. It has several digits, and if you're just getting started, it's a comfortably round place to be. From there, stash enough money to cover 3 to 6 months of living expenses. Think about all of your "must pay" costs: mortgage/rent, utilities, loans, food and a modicum of entertainment. If you are particularly worried, stretch that out and cover 12 months' expenses. Once you have three months' expenses set aside, however, breathe a little sigh of relief.

Are we done yet? No, not quite. Losing your job for economic or motivational reasons is one thing. If that happened, the aforementioned emergency account would tide you over for 3 to 6 months. You would have time to figure out how to make that stretch a little longer, too. But emergencies can get much worse. You can have a car wreck, a tornado could hit your house or you and your family could come down with a mysterious, new and expensive disease. For these sorts of things, you'll need to have cash to cover insurance deductibles and out of pocket medical expenses. Total these and add them to your monthly expense sum.

Say you have living expenses of $2,000/month with $1,000 deductible on your home and $500 on your car insurance plus a modest $2,500 deductible on your health insurance. To cover yourself for hypothetically plowing your own car into the side of your house in the sort of way that hospitalized you for 5 months, you would need:

- $2,000 x 5 = $10,000 for the bills that keep rolling in the door,
- $500 to get the car fixed and ready to go upon your release,
- $1,000 to keep your house from collapsing further,
- $2,500 to pay the good people keeping you alive
- for a total of $14,000.
- Add in another $2,000 to get yourself back on your feet once you get out of the hospital, and your new total is $16,000.

Does it have to be this way? This much money? In an account earning next to nothing?

Kind of.

That much cash sitting in an account can be very boring when it doesn't earn any interest. It can also be hard to forget about if you are tempted to spend, or you may get antsy about the returns you are missing out on elsewhere. Remember that cash has value aside from just the interest that it earns. There is value in that money being readily available and value in the assurance that it will be there should you need it.

This a very large amount of money for most people. Emergencies are, by their nature, rare. It is unlikely that you will need this money. Picture the total figure—the most conservative, totally covered amount—as a goal. You're not going to start day one with all of this saved up. You should keep this number in mind as something to build towards and as a way to restrain yourself from spending too much elsewhere.

How Do You Start Building an Emergency Fund?

Make a list of your regular monthly payments. You need a roof over your head. You need to cover the costs of transportation. You need to eat. You need to turn on the air conditioner in the summer if you're in the South and heat your home in the winter up North. You need electricity and water and garbage pickup. You need health insurance. You need to stay current on debt payments.

If after you look over your monthly expenses and you decide they're just a little more of your budget than you think they should be, then, hey, what a perfect time to start changing your lifestyle. It's probably easier to make your lifestyle more efficient NOW rather than trying to make that change when you have lost your job. Use your A/C less, ride a bike, get a roommate.

If you don't have a lot of room in your budget, start with putting aside $50 a month. Then, move up to $75. Keep inching up until you've found where you're comfortable.

If you've never practiced saving before, this can be a difficult endeavor for you. Saving is a habit. For most of us, it doesn't come naturally. Instead, we see a balance in our checking account and can find countless ways to spend it.

How Do You Make Sure It Stays Out of Your Hands and in the Bank?

Make saving automatic. Set up a monthly draft to move money from your checking account to your savings account. Before you splurge on a purchase, make yourself wait a day or two. Ask yourself a few questions: Do you need that item? If you buy it, will you still be happy with your purchase in a month? Remember your values. Does this purchase line up with them? Will it help you reach your goals? (This is a fabulous time to pull out your goals and make sure you're staying on track!) Heck, build a vision board if you need to.

Impulse buys happen to us all. Sometimes they happen when we're in line at the grocery store. Other times, we get an email about a sale and decide to load up our shopping cart with clothes we don't need. Or, we can't wait for a movie to come to Netflix, so we rent it for 24 hours on Amazon instead. Alone, these impulse buys don't amount to much. Add them all up, though, and suddenly we are looking at a pretty sizable chunk of change.

Tally up your subscriptions, too. Make sure you're getting use out of them. We're all familiar with the gym membership that never gets used, but there are plenty of other subscriptions these days that we sign ourselves up for, from video, audiobook or music streaming services to magazine and app subscriptions. Look at your account statements and make sure you are happy paying for those services every month. In most cases, there's not going to be a penalty for you to cancel now and turn around and re-subscribe later.

If you're having trouble reining in your impulses, try a change of scenery. Check out your local library. You may not be surprised to hear that there are books there, but many branches also have audio books available to check out. Other perks can include access to Ancestry.com, online courses and movies. Staying on the Internet makes online shopping an easy temptation. If you find yourself about to make a purchase, go outside for a while. Go to a park or take a walk around your neighborhood.

What Not to Use Your Emergency Fund For

Your emergency fund is not for last minute vacations or Cyber Monday sales. It's just not.

You may be thinking: Well, you said an emergency fund should cover what it costs to live, and what it costs to *really* live includes buying tickets to the NCAA College Football National Championship Game because GO TEAM. And to that, we'd like to remind you that *really* living isn't an emergency. Have a separate savings account for these types of expenses. When the account has sufficient funds, go have a blast! You need to enjoy your life. You don't want to be all ant and no grasshopper. Just make sure you are taking the funds from the appropriate account. Leave the emergency fund for emergencies. If you find yourself out of a job, you're likely to be more concerned about keeping up on your car payments so that your wheels don't get repossessed than you are about cheering for the team in person.

Remember, the emergency fund is a tool to help make your life easier and to make life's unexpected moments less traumatic. If building your emergency fund starts to stress you out, lower your monthly contribution to an amount that works for you. And breathe.

When Should You Start Building Your Emergency Fund?

The prime time to start socking away money in an emergency fund is now. The next best time is with your next paycheck.

If you don't have an emergency fund, you should prioritize this before saving the full amount for retirement with one BIG exception. If your employer offers a matching contribution on your retirement plan, at least do the required amount to get a 100% return on your money.

You may be curious and ask: Well, why does it matter if I'm saving in an emergency fund versus my retirement account? They're both mine, right? If an emergency arises and you need cash immediately, you do NOT want to have to take the money out of your retirement account. Your money is in this account to grow tax-free until you need it for retirement. Withdrawing these funds means your money isn't growing anymore, and the withdrawal is taxed AND comes with a penalty if withdrawn before you are 59 ½ (with a handful of exceptions).

You should not treat retirement accounts like savings accounts. The money needs to grow to make it less likely that you will need to look for a way to receive a paycheck when you're 80. 80 may seem like a long way off. That's great! Think of how long your money will be able to sit, invested and UNTOUCHED, growing and compounding over those decades. So, hands off. If you need to access money, look instead to that emergency fund.

If your employer doesn't offer a match, you should still contribute to a retirement plan. You can set one up yourself. Start with the monthly contribution of at least 3% of your salary. If you don't start right away when you're beginning your career, chances are you'll be pretty late to the game when you do finally get around to prioritizing retirement savings. At least do a little.

After you get your emergency fund to that magical number, it's NOT time to relax. Now you need to go back to that retirement plan and ramp it up… because 3% just isn't going to cut it!

Great Opportunities to Make Large Contributions

Contributing monthly to your emergency fund may seem like a slow go. There may be times each year when you have the opportunity to make large deposits into the account. Tax refunds, inheritance and bonuses are excellent times to make bulk contributions to your emergency fund.

If it bums you out to get that tax refund check and then turn around and put the whole thing in your emergency fund, then do what most people do: split it. Put half in savings and treat yourself with the rest. After all, you aren't just working to pay the bills. You're also working so that you have the funds to take a trip. So take a trip.

As a Wise P.I.G.G.Y. Once Said:

- Look at the real problem areas you have—those impulse spending items—whether it's eating out, clothes, books, technology, etc. Find out where you're overspending and focus on bringing those areas of expenses down.

- A rule of thumb for the size of your emergency fund advises that the amount you've saved should be enough to cover 3 to 6 months of living expenses. Of course, harking back to that time in life called the Great Recession…many people were unable to find a job that replaced the income they lost in 3 months. Start with the goal of 3 months and build from there.

- Do your best to avoid dipping into savings. Never ever borrow from your 401(k). That's a terrible thing to do.

- Once you've built your emergency cash fund, use it for emergencies. Don't use it for regular expenses.

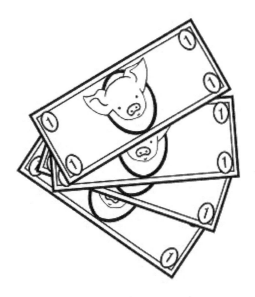

Give yourself some credit.

As a kid, you're concerned about your permanent record. Once you're an adult, you become concerned about another type of record, your credit report.

Your credit report spills all the secrets of your credit history. This tells the story of all the times in life you've said: If you give me the money now, I'll pay you back later. Your credit report reveals if you've been honest about that or not.

Why Use Credit?

A healthy credit history allows you to make the bigger purchases in life. And it costs less to borrow the money to make those purchases if you have excellent credit.

How Do You Make It Happen?

Pull your credit report. You can get three free credit reports each year from Experian, Equifax and TransUnion. These are three credit reporting agencies. You can get a report from just one of the agencies or two or all three. Once you've gotten your report, look at it—all of it. It may not be exciting, but it also shouldn't take very long (maybe five to ten minutes).

If you're just starting out, you may not have a history. You should still get a report. It's a good idea to check to make sure you haven't been the victim of identity theft.

Your report will show all the names associated with your credit. If one of these isn't you, you're probably going to want to find out who that person is and why they're affecting YOUR credit. It'll also show any previous names. Susan recently had to dispute this part of her own credit history. Sure, Susan McAdory was listed as a name on there, but it also said she was previously known as Susan Mcdory. So, she clicked a button on the report—she was viewing it online—and submitted it for dispute. Also listed are any previous addresses associated with your credit. Double-check that you've lived where it says you've lived.

If you have credit history already—for example, if you've opened a credit card or taken out a car loan—each account you've opened will be listed on the report. It will also list a variety of information on the balances, the dates the accounts were opened and closed and the status of the accounts. All of these are important pieces of information, because they are all factors in determining your credit score. In general, you don't want to carry high balances of credit card debt. The longer the account has been open, the better. And you definitely want to make payments on time.

Credit Score

Your credit score is a very important number. It's called a FICO score, which stands for Fair Isaac Corporation. This is the company that designed this scoring system. The scores range from 300 to around 800. Your score is calculated using an algorithm, or a statistical model, which basically means they use a bunch of math to figure this out. There's a great video on the Federal Reserve website about understanding your score. It's less than 10 minutes, and we recommend you watch it.

There are five main parts to your score. About 35% is going to be about your payment history. 30% will be your debt/credit ratio. 15% is the length of your credit history. 10% is the frequency with which you take out new credit. And 10% will be the types of credit.

You can see that your payment history is the largest piece of the formula. Late payments will stay on your credit record for 7 years. That's a long time for a small mistake. A bankruptcy will stay on there for 10 years. You need to pay your bills on time and in full if you don't want to mess up the payment history piece of your score.

Next, is the debt/credit ratio. This is how much you owe versus how much credit you have available to use (your credit limit). You want to keep this ratio below 50%.

Concerning the length of credit history… All of that says that you probably want to hold on to some of those old credit cards, because they will look at how long you've had that credit. The longer, the better.

The frequency of new credit… If you're one of those who loves to take advantage of those 20% offers when you stand at the register to sign up for a new card, keep in mind that overdoing it can ding your credit.

And, the types of credit… They want to see that you have a variety of loan types (a credit card, a car loan, a mortgage).

We all know that the credit score is used when taking out a loan, but did you also know that it can be looked at when you try to rent an apartment or get car insurance? (It can determine those insurance premiums.) It can even be looked at when you apply for certain jobs.

The lower your interest rate, the more house, car or stuff you can afford. Scores below 720 mean you're going to pay more on the interest rates on loans. We know that half the people out there have a score below 700, and a third have a score that's even lower than that. In the past, if you wanted to know your number, you had to pay a small fee for your score. Nowadays, there are more agencies offering the score for free, and many credit card companies will show you yours free. Remember, by law if you are turned down for credit, you are entitled to not only receive the credit report, but the free score, too. Start working on raising your credit score. It takes a long time to build up that record, and you want to keep it in pristine order.

Building Credit

If you don't have any credit history whatsoever, then you have a clean slate. Of course, since you have absolutely no history, lenders don't know for sure if you're a good bet, which means you may not qualify for the credit card with the lowest rates, no annual fee or points for days. You may have to take what you can get. If you have bad credit, you'll be less likely to qualify for those sought after cards.

Don't lose hope. You have options. You can apply for a prepaid card and use this to build credit. You can apply for a card and make payments on time and maintain a low balance and then re-negotiate with the issuer later on for lower rates after you've established better credit. You can also build credit by taking out a loan—hopefully with a low interest rate—and simply make your monthly payments on time.

Repairing Bad Credit

If you pull your credit history and notice a lot of negatives, it's time to turn the ship around. Don't keep on sailing in the wrong direction. Maybe you see that there's an account you've forgotten about – say an old phone bill that you thought you'd shut down and then let sit in the negatives for years. Pay it off as soon you can. If it seems impossible, call the company to negotiate. Make installment payments if you have to.

If you're carrying a large balance on a credit card account, make those required monthly payments on time. Try to pay extra each month if you can. Make your student loan payments on time. Make your car payments on time. Make your mortgage payments on time. You get the picture. Let time—and the consistency of your payments—work for you.

It's crucial to show that you aren't going to continue to sink further into debt. You want to show that your word is good. You said you'd pay, so you will.

Maintaining Good Credit

Once you've proven yourself a trustworthy borrower and have built up a good credit history, maybe even an excellent credit history, you'll want to stay in this sweet spot. Lenders offer you prime interest rates on debt with amazing terms, and that's not something to let fall by the wayside. Keep your credit balances low. Don't carry high balances. Make your monthly payments. Don't close credit accounts just because you're not using them. The longer an account has been open, the better. If you have good rates and no annual fee, why close that account? Even if you don't have good rates, you can probably negotiate lower ones by giving your lender a call. After ten years, credit—good and bad—rolls off your report. It's important to maintain some sort of credit activity.

Be careful about sharing a credit account with another person. If your name is attached to an account, then you are equally as responsible for payments being made on time and in full as the other person is. Make sure you have a way to monitor the account to check the balance and make payments if necessary.

Protecting Credit

Look at your account activity. There's really no excuse not to know what's happening in your checking and credit card accounts. All of your transactions can be viewed online. Look at them. Get an app and categorize them. Know where your money is going. If something looks suspicious, investigate it. The sooner, the better. Set up alerts on your accounts to send you a text or an email if a charge is made on your account. Review your credit report at least once a year (www.annualcreditreport.com). Remember, you can get one every 365 days from each of the credit agencies. This means you can request one every year—say on your birthday—from all three. Or, you can stagger them. Maybe get the one from Experian on Valentine's Day, Equifax on Independence Day and TransUnion on Halloween. Your choice. Review your report. Does everything check out? If not, you can put in a dispute online, over the phone or by snail mail.

If during this review process, you realize your identity has been stolen, your next step is to file an identity theft report. You will likely file this with your local police department. Once this report has been filed, you can place a 7 year fraud victim alert to your credit report. You will need a copy of the police report you filed along with other information. You will want to alert any company you have an account with to let them know that your identity has been compromised (credit cards, bank accounts, loans, etc.). Continue to review your account statements from checking and savings accounts, credit card accounts, loans, investments, etc. If you see a charge or other activity you don't recognize, investigate it.

If you've been the victim of identity theft in the past—or if you're so worried you will be that you're losing sleep—you have a couple of options. If you are moderately concerned, you can place a 90 day fraud alert on your credit report with one of the three credit reporting agencies. You only need to place this fraud alert with one of the agencies, because that agency will then alert the other two. After you place this fraud alert, you will receive a free credit report from the credit reporting agency where you placed the initial fraud alert. Review this report. If you see something you don't recognize (for example, a credit card account you didn't open, an address you never lived at, someone requesting your credit report without your approval), alert the agency immediately and file a report. Once this report has been filed, you can place a 7 year fraud victim alert to your credit report.

If you are extremely concerned, place a security freeze on ALL THREE of your credit reports. You will have to do this at each of the separate companies: Equifax, Experian and TransUnion. If you can prove that you were the victim of identity theft, then you will usually be able to place the freeze for free. Otherwise, there is a fee (around $10) which varies by state. Depending on whether or not you were the victim of identity theft and can provide the necessary documentation to show it, you may or may not have to pay a fee each time you'd like to temporarily lift the credit freeze or when you'd like to permanently remove the credit freeze. Each time you'd like to lift the freeze or remove the freeze, you will need a PIN number, which is created when you place the initial freeze. Do your utmost not to lose or forget this PIN number.

A credit freeze requires that each time a request is made on your history—be it to open a credit card account or to take out a loan, etc.—the credit agency will give you a call and require you to provide them with a long PIN number to prove that you authorized the pull on your credit. This isn't something everyone wants or needs. It can be a hassle.

NOTE: Fraud alerts do not prevent you from requesting a free annual credit report from each of the credit reporting agencies.

As a Wise P.I.G.G.Y. Once Said:

- Pull your credit reports yearly.

- Clean up old bills on your credit report.

- Pay bills in full and on time!

- Keep credit card balances low.

- Keep some old credit cards to show a long credit history.

- Be careful about sharing a credit account with someone.

- Monitor your credit. Be on the lookout for identity theft.

- Stop impulse spending!

- Do not put more on your credit card than you can afford to pay off each month.

Advice that has Stood the Test of Time

Nancy's Column from 1999:

Recently, I heard an economist state that Americans spend, on average, 105% of their income. Surely, I misunderstood. I asked him to repeat the statement. He stated that Americans spend, on average, 105% of their income.

How do you spend 5% more than what you have coming in? Simple. Just say, "Charge it."

Americans have become a debt-laden society. We don't just live from paycheck to paycheck anymore. We live from minimum payment to minimum payment. Our standard of living is higher than our parents, but we are living on the edge. Bankruptcy is one small missed payment away and planning for the future is totally out of mind.

Our parents sacrificed and deprived themselves to give us everything we wanted. And we have learned our lessons well. We have bigger homes, fancier cars and more gadgets than we know what to do with. We eat microwave dinners and drink instant coffee. Life in the fast lane has led us to expect instant gratification. And we wonder why our children are so spoiled.

There is a push in our society to live on credit. Every day, I receive solicitations in the mail for credit cards. All I have to do is sign on the bottom line and return a card. I get "checks" in the mail that are actually cash advances. Just sign and I'll have all the cash I need.

Each night, our dinner is interrupted by telemarketers offering another avenue of credit. Every time I sign onto my computer, I see a dazzling screen offering me credit.

The message is that there is no end to the availability of money. It's a bottomless pit.

It's a pit, all right. A deep, dark, can't-get-out-of-it-with-a-bulldozer pit. Spend yourself into debt because you can't wait one more minute for that thing that you just can't live without. That thing that ends up in the back corner of your closet. Instant gratification leaves you empty and can leave you in deep financial trouble.

One Step Too Far

And now, the final blow: The IRS has just announced they will start taking payments for taxes by credit card. And they (your payment processor) will charge you an extra fee for doing it. This is insanity. All the government is doing is putting the collection burden on the credit card companies. And these companies are more than willing to take this on because of the big interest payments they'll receive.

Some people say charging your taxes is better than having your wages garnished. Some people say you can use your tax bill to build up frequent flyer miles.

Some people say this will stop those awful IRS agents from going overboard.

I say hogwash!

Paying taxes is a civic responsibility. It is not an unexpected expense. It is a certainty. The very people who will take advantage of credit cards to pay their taxes are the ones least able to afford to do this. This will only delay the inevitable and exacerbate their situations.

Over the last two weeks, I have met with two families with similar situations. Both had an aging parent. Both families thought of their upbringing as "meager." Both talked of their hard-working, self-sacrificing parents. And both sets of children were shocked to learn their parents had managed to tuck away hundreds of thousands of dollars on limited incomes.

They lived on less than 100% of their income and saved the rest. Their homes were paid for. Their cars were paid for. They used credit cards sparingly and wisely.

There is a lesson to be learned here. 100% is more than enough for anyone.

Learn how to use other people's money to get things done.

Debt

No surprise here: debt is something you owe. The longer you take to repay that debt, the more it costs you. As they say, time is money. Pretending it's not there will not make it go away. Instead, learn to use debt in a reasonable way. We call that "leverage." Like a lever, debt can make it easier to manage a heavy load, but it can also crush you like a giant boulder rolling downhill if you don't watch out.

If we're just looking at debt as money, then your debt comes from someone who has extra money. Those people with extra money don't need to spend it and don't want to spend it, but they also don't want it hanging out there just sitting pretty. They'd rather their extra money turn into more money. Smart, right? So instead of sitting on the money, they "sell" or lend it to someone who doesn't have enough money to buy what she wants. They put a price on this money and a price on the time it takes for them to see this money back in their own pockets. The price of money is known as interest or return.

How is that Price Set?

The amount you have to fork over in interest each month depends on a handful of factors including:

- the amount you're looking to borrow,

- how long it will take you to pay that amount back,

- how frequently you will make payments,

- whether or not the debt is backed up by some form of collateral,

- and whether or not you have a respectable history of repaying debt in the past.

All of these factors boil down to this: This debt...are you good for it? That's where your credit history comes into play. Your credit report shows just how risky you really are.

Interest Rates

We can't talk about interest rates without talking about inflation. There are two types of rates: nominal and real. The nominal rate is the raw number for the interest rate. In the 1980s, the nominal rate for mortgages hit 18% and the nominal rate for a 2 year certificate of deposit was about 12%. In 2017, the nominal rate for mortgages was about 4%, and the nominal rate for a 2 year CD was about 1.5%—big difference.

Most people get hung up on the raw number. They say: Wow, I'd love to have those CD rates from the 80s again! Or they think: Mortgage rates are really low today. Nominal rates mean very little if you don't think about inflation.

When we subtract inflation from the nominal rate, we get the "real" interest rate. The "real" number tells us about the purchasing power of our money. Right now, inflation is very low, so the rates we are seeing are closer to being "real," whereas if we subtract inflation in the 80s from the nominal rate, it will look more like today's rates. In the 1980s, inflation was about 14%. Subtract that from the 1980s mortgage of 18%, and you're back to a 4% mortgage. Reduce a 12% CD rate by inflation in 1980, and you end up with a -2% rate. It's not an exact science, but it comes close.

While nominal rates fluctuate widely, real rates are more stable. Most of the difference in rates across the decades can be accounted for by looking at inflation. That doesn't mean we ignore the nominal rate. It means we understand that when CD rates and savings account rates are high, inflation is probably high as well.

Smart borrowers will note the changes in nominal rates and use them to their advantage. Low mortgage rates? Great time to buy a house! High CD rates? Might want to lock in for a longer period of time. Ultimately, this all comes out in the wash, in the long run. But in the shorter runs, smart borrowers lock in debt at low rates and smart lenders lock in loans at high rates.

Revolving Debt vs. Installment Debt

Credit cards, loans, mortgages… You can rack up debt in different ways and for different things.

Credit cards are a form of revolving debt. There's a limit on how much you can spend, but your balance may vary from month to month. Unless you're a champ and pay off your balance in full each month, your required monthly payment will go up or down depending on how much you still owe. Be a champ.

Credit cards can be a useful tool to manage your spending and cash flow, but you should never use them to buy something that you cannot actually afford to pay for in cash. There are financial and not-exactly-financial benefits to owning credit cards, but it's easy to run into financial trouble if you don't keep a close eye on what you're doing. Even if you only spend what you can afford, missing payment dates or stretching out your payments can lead to fees and excessive interest costs. Mistakes will bring down that precious credit score of yours.

Sometimes it's not possible to pay off that credit card each month. You might have an unexpected big expense and not enough in your emergency fund to cover the bill. Don't panic. Make a plan to pay it off in 3 to 4 months. Avoid charging anything else until you get that balance down to zero.

Unlike revolving debt, installment debt has set monthly payments and a set schedule for paying off the loan. Think of a car loan or a mortgage… or maybe even a furniture or computer loan. Agreeing to an installment loan is a commitment. While you can pay the minimum on a credit card if you get in a pinch, you don't have that option with an installment loan. Instead, you must pay the agreed upon monthly amount. Otherwise, you might lose the house, the car, the computer; and you'll definitely wreck your credit.

Back to credit cards…

Which Card is Best for You?

Remember, the price of money is interest. If you're buying, you want to pay less. When it comes to credit cards, it makes sense you would choose the card with the lowest interest rate, right? Well, it depends.

First, ask yourself: Will I pay off the bill in full every month? If the answer is yes, then you don't care about the interest rate. That's because those interest charges don't kick in until after the bill is due. While some people pay their bills in full each month, not everyone does. In fact, most people don't. But for those who do, the interest rate on the card is irrelevant. There are other things that are important to them when it comes to choosing a card. We'll get to those in a minute.

For those who let those charges carry over from month to month, interest rates are critical. Lower is better, because those interest charges may eventually get charged on OTHER interest charges. That's where you can get into trouble. If this sounds like you, then you need to shop for the lowest interest rate you can get.

But don't forget fees: annual fees, late fees, transaction fees and what the fee is based on. These can vary from card to card. Read the fine print in the contract.

Understand that the competition in the credit card business is fierce. With that in mind, should you really be paying an annual fee? It makes since only if there is some prize worth more than the fee. Do you get a companion airline ticket or discounts at restaurants? Whatever the enticement, make sure it's of value to YOU, and make sure it's easy to redeem. Otherwise, forget it. It costs more than it's worth.

Finally, check out the cashback system or reward points. What works best for you? Know that card companies can change their offerings, so the card with the best points now may not be the best for you later.

Ultimately, your best defense in navigating the credit card business is to have a great credit score. If your score is good, they'll be throwing all kinds of goodies at you to get you to sign up. Have a credit problem? You may end up paying higher annual fees and interest charges to get anyone to give you an account.

Is Debt a Bad Thing?

All debt isn't all bad. Some debts are even good.

Student loan debt, for example, is an investment in future earning potential. The interest rates aren't outrageous, and borrowers have a generous amount of time to repay the loans. Rates are set by Congress, so you can know ahead of time what you should expect to pay and plan accordingly.

Many of us depend on auto loans to buy our transportation. Without a car loan, Susan would've been in quite the pickle one week into her job with us. When an 18-wheeler totaled her 13 year old Ford, the driver didn't check with her first to see if she'd saved up enough to replace it. She used the insurance check, which covered the value of her Ford at the time of the wreck, for an upfront payment and took out a loan for the remaining cost of the replacement vehicle, paying around 4% in interest.

Before you head into a dealership, it's a good idea to go online and look at current rates. This way you'll know what you should expect to agree to in your loan contract.

Mortgages allow homebuyers another way to invest in their future selves. We spend a large chunk of our income on housing. With a mortgage, you're spending that money on a place you'll own rather than a place someone else owns.

And, business debt can make perfect sense if it lets you earn more in the future.

Good debt may have low interest rates, may give you a tax break or may be an investment in your future.

What about bad debt? Bad debt would be most revolving debt, otherwise known as consumer debt. This means credit cards. Bad debt is expensive.

It has a high interest rate, and instead of helping you move forward, it only serves to drag you down.

Credit cards are usually an expensive debt to hold because banks charge a pretty high interest rate. Using a credit card versus a debit card, however, typically provides greater protection from identity theft. It's easy to dispute a charge—the credit card company will oftentimes launch their own investigation into cases of fraud—and you are likely to be reimbursed for any fraudulent charges. When banking information is stolen from your debit card (or your check…), the stakes are higher. A thief has immediate access to your cash balance. Depending on your bank, you may or may not be reimbursed, and there is usually a smaller time frame for you to report the theft to your bank in order to qualify for repayment. When you spend money with your debit card, you're spending YOUR money. When you spend money with your credit card, you're spending the credit card company's money.

How Do You Pay Down Debt?

Make it a habit to pay your credit card balance each month in full. Just because you CAN spend up to your limit, this doesn't mean you SHOULD. Say you have three cards with a spending limit of $10k. If you only make $3,000 a month but max your cards out on a shopping spree, you'll be paying pretty dearly for that debt.

Make your regular payments on time. It isn't worth it to be late, and it dings your credit history.

Prioritize paying down high interest rate debt, because that is your most expensive debt.

Dealing With Too Much Debt

When we use a credit card, we tend to spend more, and that transaction creates debt that we're going to have to deal with later. What can you do? The first thing is to make a plan to pay everything off. List each balance.

List the interest rate on each card. Start with those low balance cards first just to give yourself a sense of accomplishment, and then concentrate on the high interest cards. The really hard part is, unless it's an absolute emergency, don't put any more on that credit card. Your goal should be to pay off those credit cards before next Christmas. If you do that, the payments you're making on the credit cards can now go into savings to build an emergency fund or a Christmas fund for next year.

For most of us, we do need to have a credit card, because so many transactions, especially if you're doing them online, require a card. Even though a debit card doesn't create debt, a credit card gives you more protection in case someone takes your identity or takes that card. You can immediately let the credit card company know that you did not participate in the transaction and that money does not come out. If it's a debit card, you may have to go through months of wrangling to get that money put back in.

Debt Hangover

The debt hangover can be hard to get over. Right now, for people who are carrying debt, the average household credit card debt is around $15,000. That's a lot. The average interest rate on those credit cards is 15%, but if you have poor credit those rates could be up to 30% which makes it an almost impossible hole to climb out of. The average number of credit cards per household is four. With four, we can juggle debt and fool ourselves into thinking we don't owe that much. Once we add them all up, though, we see the damage.

How do you cure that hangover? Well, not with the hair of the dog. You have to do it the hard way. Collect all of your statements. Set up a table and really get it in front of you. List every account and list every balance so the numbers are right there in your face. List the interest rate on each card and the minimum payment.

Then, you need to ask the question: How much can I afford out of my household budget to apply to paying down those credit cards each month?

You need to pay the minimum on each card except for one. We usually tell people to start with the small balances, because paying it off will be a little victory you can celebrate. Then, get rid of the high interest credit cards, and just work your way down one card at a time. Once you get rid of one card, that money you were paying on it can apply to the next one. Know that if you have overindulged for years, it may take years to correct; but if it's just a holiday hiccup, you should be able to clear it out in three to four months. If you fall off the wagon, just get back on.

Also, consider a balance transfer card for relief. Often they will offer a 0% interest rate for a teaser period. Just mark your calendar, because those rates will go up afterwards. That introductory rate will disappear to be replaced by a much higher rate. Federal law requires these companies to keep that low rate for at least 6 months. Most charge a fee, an average of 3%, just to do the transfer. Look for companies with lower transfer fees and longer introductory periods to take advantage of the time to clean up your credit. Whatever you do, don't get caught with a big balance when the intro period ends.

Remember that the key to a financially healthy you is to get rid of credit card debt. Until you get your spending under control and make a habit of living within your means, you'll struggle to save and to invest. With a little discipline and a little time, you can knock it out. It's a great feeling to be in control of your money, because that money is going to give you more room in your budget to enjoy life and to save for the bigger things down the road.

Debt Hazards: Bankruptcy and Protecting Your Assets

An asset is what you *own*; a liability is what you *owe*. After you've built up your assets, the question is: What happens if you have a lawsuit against you or if you declare bankruptcy?

Bankruptcy is a last resort. It's what happens when you can't even make the minimum payments on your bills. It is designed to give you some relief.

After all, we no longer have debtors' prisons. Instead, we recognize that sometimes we just need to start over.

There are two types of personal bankruptcy. One is really a slowdown, and it's known as Chapter 13. The court steps in and helps you regroup, stretch out your payments and eventually pay off your bills. Minimum payments get adjusted. Maturity dates of debt get delayed. Creditors have to agree to all terms for this to happen.

Chapter 7 is more severe. Some debt gets wiped out, but you can end up losing a lot.

Bankruptcy is governed by state laws and most offer some protection for your home. Each state is different. Texas and Florida are the most generous in protecting those houses up to a certain amount. When it comes to bankruptcy, you can only keep a certain dollar amount of equity, or ownership, of the house. This doesn't mean value. It means what you own. Be careful with that. There can be some protection of your house in a lawsuit depending on the ownership. What you might want to consider is an umbrella liability insurance policy to protect all those assets you've built up; but read the fine print, because there could be limitations on the policy.

You may also get protection for your retirement plans. We're always encouraging people to save for retirement anyway. This is an extra plus. If you have a lawsuit or bankruptcy, you have some protections for those 401(k)s, IRAs, 403(b)s, etc. Know that they're still not protected from the Feds. So, if you owe taxes, they can still stick their hands in those funds. And, if you owe child support, those accounts will not be protected.

This does not apply to all inherited IRAs. If you inherit an IRA from a spouse, you are protected. But, for instance, if you have a parent who dies, and they pass on an IRA to you, then that account *can* be accessed.

529 Education Plans are also protected. Here in Mississippi, we call that the MACS or MPACT Plan. So, if you put money into this plan for a child, you'll have some protection against lawsuits and bankruptcy.

What if you own a business? Many people will incorporate a business for protection. An S Corporation or an LLC (a Limited Liability Corporation) offers some protection against lawsuits and could help you keep your personal assets separate from the business.

Remember, retirement accounts are protected in many ways, so save for retirement and protect your assets at the same time! Your house gives you limited protections. Regardless, while bankruptcy isn't death, it does wreck your credit. It may take you 7-10 years to overcome this mark on your report, so handle debt with care!

As a Wise P.I.G.G.Y. Once Said:

- Good debt is low interest debt that allows you to produce more in the future.

- Bad debt is consumer debt (credit cards, et al.). If you can't afford to pay off the card at the end of the month, don't pull out the card.

- Choose a credit card that matches your spending habits. Keep the interest and fees low and the cashback and rewards points high.

- If you have a credit hangover, set up a payment plan to deal with it. Prioritize paying off high interest rate cards.

- Bankruptcy should be a last resort. It will give you relief now but will wreck your credit for years to come.

Earn money.

Why Work?

You know why you work. You work because you have to. Because you want a pocket of the world to call your own. Animals have nests and dens, but you want 2000 square feet and a porch swing. You want hot showers, fresh food and fast Internet, and none of that is free. You have to work for it.

You have to get out there and do something for thirty to forty years of your life that, if we're honest with ourselves, most of us probably wouldn't still be doing if we won the lottery. If we're lucky, we land a solid job with decent pay and people we like. We pay off our student loans and go on trips and buy houses. We get checkups and fix our teeth and stay home when we're sick. And one day we can even afford to stop working.

If you plan well, you may have the opportunity to do something you love. Maybe not right away, of course, but on down the line. You can start your own business and work for yourself. Or you can help shape the company or your position into your dream job. Enjoying the work you do is immensely rewarding, partly because we spend so much of our lives working. Knowing that you do good work that has a positive impact with people you like is almost priceless, and it's definitely a career goal to strive for.

What's Worth Your While?

The time you spend working is time you aren't spending doing whatever you'd want to be doing if money was no object. It's a tradeoff. Some of your time for the ability to get something you need: food, shelter, security...personal time, quiet, a beach view. Things you need to get by and things you need to be happy. You just have to figure out whether the tradeoff is worth it—whether your job makes you happy enough.

Of course, that's what we're all after, right? Happiness. Satisfaction. Joy. We don't all need the exact same things to reach this "happy enough" state of being, though. We're all snowflakes. Take the time to imagine your life in five or ten or forty years. What kind of life do you see yourself living during those different stages of your life?

Understand that the income you earn will directly impact the life you lead. The choices you make while you're young can be a huge part of how free you are to fund your adult life.

One strong indicator of earnings potential is the level of education you achieve. Reaching higher levels of education translates into higher pay and lower unemployment rates. The Bureau of Labor Statistics reports for 2015 that the median weekly earnings for all workers is $860, and it's not until you earn a bachelor's degree or above that the median earnings are above that $860 a week. Those with professional or doctoral degrees are more likely to earn double that. Associate's degrees, incomplete college degrees, high school diplomas and incomplete high school education all earn on average less than the $860 a week. Those who fail to earn a high school diploma typically earn less than $500 each week.

Conversely, unemployment rates follow the trend of rising the less education you complete. The BLS report averages the unemployment rate in 2015 for all workers in the U.S. at 4.3%. Those with an associate's degree, bachelor's degree or above have a lower unemployment rate, while those with no degree are more likely to be unemployed. Failing to complete a college degree puts you in the 5% unemployment rate category. Failing to complete a high school education bumps you to an 8% unemployment rate!

However, salaries and unemployment rates also vary greatly depending on your choice of major and how well-suited your abilities are to that major. If math is far from your strong suit, barely completing a degree in statistics without achieving a proficiency in the subject is unlikely to translate into the average salary for that major. Remember, the average salary isn't a given. It's just an average. Some people will earn much more than that and vice versa.

Likewise your choice of schools can play a part in all of this. Be curious about potential careers and the work they entail. Put in the effort before you decide on a major and a school. You may learn during your time in college or through an internship that although you can do a job, you would much rather make a change and pursue a different career goal. The earlier you find this out the better. So do the legwork. Look at the latest studies comparing earnings by degrees and schools. The Georgetown University Center on Education and the Workforce produces a number of reports to help you plan for your future.

Again, ask yourself what kind of life you want to lead. Then, do your research and figure out a plan to get there.

What to Look for in a Job

Salary

You're definitely going to want to get paid for the work you do. I think we'd be hard-pressed to find many people with a cap on how much they'd be willing to accept for their efforts, but most of us probably have an idea of how much we need to earn to cover our expenses. However, after that we differ. A lucrative career with high earnings potential may be the dream for one person while work that contributes to the community through a nonprofit may be the goal for another. The type of work you do and the sector you do that work in will determine what type of pay you should expect. Working for a nonprofit often does not offer the same earnings as corporate work.

Expect your salary to vary based on your geographic location. Compare salaries for your industry and position in various regions. This will let you know whether you're being offered a fair salary and to negotiate a better deal for yourself.

If you're looking for your first job out of college, lower your expectations. That median earnings by major report you researched may show that the average salary for someone with your degree is $60,000, but be mindful of whether this data pertains to starting salaries or earnings over the course of the career. If you just graduated, you're most likely an entry level employee, and you will need to prove your competency and usefulness. Expect to earn significantly less in an entry level position than you will after fifteen years of accomplishments.

Raises and Promotions

If you're working for a large company or the government, raises may be fairly strict and follow a set time schedule. Often raises and promotions can be expedited the higher your level of education. A master's degree, for instance, may equal an additional year of experience, and a doctoral may equal more. Smaller or faster growth companies may offer raises and promotions depending upon individual performance and contribution. If you're in sales, you may earn a base salary and the rest of your earnings may come from commissions.

Time

Your time is valuable to both you and to your employer. It's a good idea to know how much of it your career will likely demand of you. Some fields of work simply require a certain understood time commitment. Tax accountants know January to April is a far cry from a forty-hour work week. Teachers know that all of the work isn't done in the classroom— some of it gets taken home in the form of lesson planning, grading homework and responding to concerned parents. Production jobs require weekend shifts if the company falls behind. Retail is busy on the holidays when other jobs are off.

Take the time to imagine what your ideal work schedule would look like, and remember to consider how much vacation time you'd like available. You're unlikely to get your dream schedule right away, but it's something to work towards. Know going into your line of work whether the job will be a good fit for you and how you'd like to spend your time. After all, each of us has a limited amount of it. Go back and look at what's most important to you, and use your values to help you decide on the type of work to pursue.

Health Insurance

You need it. The whole point of insurance is to manage risk, and your health is a big risk. It's also an expensive risk. Having an employer who covers the cost of your health insurance is similar to earning a higher salary.

If your employer covers your health insurance for you, visit the government exchange and get an idea of what you would otherwise be paying if the company didn't cover you. Now add that monthly amount onto your salary. You're making that, too.

Retirement Savings

Another extra earnings consideration is retirement savings. Not all jobs offer retirement plans. This is another benefit some companies provide to their employees. Retirement plans come in all shapes and sizes. Some companies offer a match, meaning if you contribute a certain percentage, they'll match your contribution up to a point. Sometimes the match is time-based. After you work there a year, they'll match 1%, two years, 2%, three years, 3%...up to whatever that company's cap may be. That's extra money you're earning! Preparing for retirement is vital and almost entirely on your shoulders, not the company's. Take the time to educate yourself on the topic, and take advantage of whatever help your company may offer, because you're likely going to need it.

Professional Growth Opportunities

One perk some companies offer is professional development. You may have some or all of graduate coursework covered. You may be encouraged to work towards one or more professional certifications that will set you apart in your industry. You may be sent to conferences to learn the latest trends and technologies. If your position at the company supports any or all of these opportunities, it's a sign that the company is willing to invest in its workers' careers. You become a more highly skilled employee with a higher earning potential. Even if your time at the company comes to an end at some point (hopefully amicably), your master's degree, certification or proficiency at new technology goes with you and makes you more valuable (and more likely to get hired) at your next job.

Companies may add an additional area of professional development: networking. Though it's unlikely that your boss will cover every club you want to be a part of, you may find that you work for a company that promotes networking and will cover fees and membership dues. At no cost to you, then, you're able to expand your professional network, which could end up landing you your next client, reference or even your next job.

Earn money.

Flexibility

For most of us, life throws us a few curveballs, and our day-to-day gets hectic for a while. We get sick. Sometimes we get really sick. We start families. Our families get sick, and we have to take care of them. We have car trouble. Our pets get hurt. We get divorced. And sometimes we realize we just need some time away for our sanity.

Whatever hiccups or hurdles come along to throw you off your daily routine, it definitely makes dealing with them easier if you have a job that offers you the flexibility in your work schedule to properly handle them. Not all jobs can be as flexible, of course, but it is a feature of potential jobs to consider. Having that extra room in your schedule if you need it is a huge benefit.

Company Culture

Do you like the people you work with? Many people consider this to be one of the most important aspects of a job. We spend a lot of time at work which means we spend a lot of time with our coworkers. While you probably shouldn't expect to like everyone, you definitely don't want to be miserable at the office. Consider how much privacy the job offers you in your day-to-day routine and whether that's enough for you.

Along those same lines, you'll want to keep in mind what's expected of you as far as production goes. In some positions, going the extra mile may be expected and rewarded. You may do well if you're competitive and ambitious. However, other positions focus more on teamwork and the delegation of duties. Trying to do more than you're expected may end up with little payoff and a lot of stress. You don't want to exhaust yourself with efforts that will only lead to burnout. You're just one person after all. Do your job, and do it well, but don't put it on yourself to do everyone else's job. This isn't to say you won't be asked to do more from time to time. We all are. A company that recognizes and rewards productivity and creativity is a company you want to work for.

Miscellaneous Perks

Some jobs come with other perks that save you a monthly bill. Paying your monthly phone bill or covering a gym membership translates into money you're getting to pocket each month. Companies may also stock the kitchen at the office, or your boss may treat you to lunch. These miscellaneous benefits are great, but probably aren't going to be what makes you choose one offer over another. However, they do help to make you feel valued in your position. And not to be too cliché, but when your work is valued, well, you value your work.

When to Start Looking

It's really never too early to start looking at companies you might want to work for or open positions you're interested in. You may not have any idea of what type of work you'd like to do. If you're in that boat, go online and look at open positions around the country. The job description will give you an idea of that job's responsibilities and the qualifications necessary to be considered. If you're early in your college career, this can be a useful way to help you decide on your major.

If you know the industry you'd like to work in, learn about some of the companies in it and apply for internships (if you're still in college—this is generally a requirement). Familiarity with an industry and the companies it's made up of—particularly the company you want to work for—is expected if you want to land the job.

Much of the time, we can also expect to move to accept a position. This might just be a couple of hours away, or the move may take us to the opposite coast. Distance aside, when you're looking at potential jobs or trying to decide what direction to pursue in your career, it'd be a bit negligent not to consider location in your job search.

Some people are really against moving. Sure, their ancestors uprooted, crossed an ocean and traversed the country, but by golly this is their town and they're sticking around. We get it. We are all from Mississippi, and we are all still in Mississippi. We may have left a time or two and for a few years, but the South kept calling us back home. If you want to stay a local, though, it behooves you to be curious about your potential job opportunities. Get to know your professors. Make local connections. Network. Make an impression (a good one). You want people to keep you in mind if they hear about a job opening. There's no better endorsement than having someone say: I know the perfect person for that job. You should call Ryder!

Not everyone wants to stick around their hometown. If you have a specific location in mind, find out who's hiring and which companies are located there. Apply for a summer internship in the area.

If you've already taken a position, but you have the feeling it's not a company you see yourself working for over the long haul, keep tabs on open positions elsewhere. You may not see a job you want to try for at first, but if you keep open positions on your radar, you won't miss an opportunity that presents itself. Remember, though, not to job surf while you're actually at work. Your employer can check your browsing history, and it really doesn't bode well for you if your boss finds out you've been sending out your résumé while you're on the clock.

When to Reassess

Many companies offer periodic employee reviews. It's a good practice to prepare for yours beforehand. Keep a running list throughout the year of contributions you've made or suggestions you have for the company and your position. Most of us would be hard-pressed to come up with a comprehensive list of a year's worth of achievements off the tops of our heads. An email draft or a note on your phone helps you keep track. Maybe it's a big client you brought in or a project you've helped move along. Write it down and bring it up in your review. This will help you negotiate for more. Whether you want a bonus, a raise, a promotion or more time off, you'll be more likely to get it if you come prepared and can back up your requests.

Keep your goals in mind when you're negotiating. Sure, you're asking for more for yourself and your needs, but you're also asking for more for the people who depend on you: your spouse, your kids, etc. And your pets bring you a lot of joy, but they also come with their fair share of expenses. If you're looking to add a kitten to your life, add some padding to your budget. He's going to need more trips to the vet than you think.

Most of the time we don't start out with our dream jobs. We work a number of jobs and learn what we like doing and what we definitely don't like doing. Your first job likely won't be your last, but that doesn't mean you can't learn from it and build yourself professionally while you're there. A lot of jobs still come from networking. It's who you know not what you know, right? Although some of us are lucky enough to stumble upon a great job, most of the time good jobs don't find you, you find them. So keep your eyes open.

Advice for Graduates

The jobs search is a numbers game. The more times you apply, the more your chances grow. It's a competitive world out there, so don't take it personally if you get turned down.

Show up early; don't just show up on time. Dress appropriately, and stay off Facebook and Twitter (unless that's part of your job). Be happy you have a job, because it's still very tough out there! Know your benefits. Pay attention to what's being offered by your employer beyond just the salary. Sign up for that 401(k) as soon as you can, and immediately start contributing at least 10% of your paycheck. Get started as soon as you can, and that will pay off down the road.

Make sure you have a good résumé. Any kind of experience, whether it's volunteer experience or part-time jobs that you've had while in school, will help. Just know that employers are looking. They're looking for competent people with good work ethics. Show them you're excited to have a job and that you want to be there, and you'll be in good shape to find a place to work.

Earn money.

In many ways, a great career is like respect: it's not given, it's earned. When you're hired, your employer is giving you that initial chance. Now it's your turn to use that opportunity to earn your place and prove your worth to the company. Show them what you can do. You have no idea just how impressive competence and a pleasant demeanor are in the workplace. If you can do your job well and make the workplace a better place to be five days a week, you're on your way.

As a Wise P.I.G.G.Y. Once Said:

- Get a good education!

- Research salaries for your degree and vocation.

- Don't forget the "benefit" of that benefits package.

- Know what's important in your work life.

- Network. Network. Network.

- Getting a job is a numbers game. Keep applying!

- When you get the job, don't blow it. Show up on time, and earn your place.

Pay your dues.

Taxes

Griping about taxes is a proud American ritual. It takes up more of our time than preparing for the Super Bowl, celebrating the Fourth of July and comparing our state to neighboring states combined. It takes slightly less of our time than the presidential election season. We gripe about taxes for good reason—they are complicated to do. Even if you don't owe much, or anything, the process of doing your own taxes may seem daunting. Many people hand off this arduous task to a CPA or another tax preparer so that they don't have to deal with it.

While we encourage everyone to take a stab at doing their taxes by hand at least once, there are plenty of tools out there to help you through the process. If you don't want anything to do with the process, you can pay someone to do them for you. Just a quick note of caution when hiring someone else: there are no qualifications to be a tax preparer. While there are plenty of people who can do your taxes, there is no minimum qualification required by the IRS nor is there any regulation of the field. You are on your own here.

Our advice is to look to a reputable shop that is open year round (there are always plenty of fly-by-night places around this time of year) or turn to a CPA (a Certified Public Accountant). CPAs are highly qualified accountants who are best prepared for larger or more complicated returns. Bear in mind they will be more expensive but worth it if you are not doing it yourself.

Step One

Take a couple of deep breaths. Doing your taxes is probably less complicated than you think. No pressure, but it is also your civic duty as an American.

Step Two

Gather all of your documents. Any mail you have received that says "important tax documents enclosed" probably has something relevant to the process. You should expect to have a tax form for every financial account you have: bank accounts that earn interest, brokerage accounts, retirement accounts, loans, etc. You will also have a tax form from every source of income: jobs, freelance or contracted work. The most common, most important information is as follows:

- Work/Income - How much did you earn? How much tax was paid on your behalf?

- Bank Accounts - How much interest did you earn?

- Retirement Accounts - How much did you contribute or withdraw?

- Brokerage Accounts - Did you realize any gains or losses this past year?

- Mortgage and Student Loans - How much interest did you pay?

Those documents should show up in your inbox or mailbox by mid-February.

Also, gather documents on rental income you received or businesses you own. There are a slew of income sources and deductible expenses listed by the IRS that you can walk through to determine whether or not they apply to you.

You will also need to know if you are married or if you had any children in your possession last year. Generally speaking, if you possessed a child for more than half of the year, you get to claim them as a dependent.

Step Three

This is a good time to learn the lingo. If you have a regular job that has benefits and withholds taxes from your paycheck, you will have a W-2 from them. Your contract employers, banks and brokerage firms will send you a 1099. These both show types of income. The main filing form is called a 1040, and you report more details for that on your Schedule C, D or E. Be careful, though, if you are self-employed as you will need the 1040 Schedule SE. If you paid tuition last year or are claiming an education credit, you will need to fill out Form 8917 or 8863. If you have a low income and a large family, you will want to check on Schedule EIC. If your household help considers you their employer, check out Schedule H; and if you paid taxes to a foreign government, you might get that back on Form 1116.

All of these forms are available on www.IRS.gov, and paper copies are available at local libraries, by request or through your own printer. The core filing is the Form 1040. All other forms and schedules come off of that.

Step Four

Take another deep breath. Remember, the maintenance of the Republic is in your hands here.

Step Five

Decide the best route for filing your taxes. If you don't have a lot of forms—maybe just a W-2 from work and a 1099 from your bank showing $11 in interest—you could do this easily yourself by hand. Online programs like TurboTax or H&R Block can walk you through the process fairly efficiently if you have all of your documents gathered. You typically get a free filing for simple returns at lower incomes. If you don't qualify for a free filing, these online tools can still help you figure out what you owe and what to put on a paper filing.

If you have more complicated taxes, particularly if you own a business, you may want to turn to a CPA. A CPA will typically not only provide the most accurate filing for you, but can also offer tax advice on how you can reduce your taxes with expenses you incurred in the previous year or by maximizing contributions to a retirement account appropriate for your work situation.

Let's imagine that you are filing by hand for the rest of this chapter.

Step Six

Start walking down the Form 1040. You will learn to love this form. Or not. Maybe you won't. If you truly love America, you probably will though.

Here are the only instructions you will need for doing your taxes: Read each line carefully and ask yourself (or the instructions) if it applies to you. Fill it out appropriately and move to the next line. Repeat. If you want something more detailed than that, the IRS helpfully offers instructions for each of their forms. While they aren't always the easiest to read, they are broken out line by line, so just focus on the line at hand.

Let's Start at the Top

Start with your name. If you are married, you will typically file jointly with your spouse. Times when you would not are if one spouse had lots of deductible expenses and a significantly lower income than the other spouse. You can figure out further down the line if this makes sense for you to file jointly, but for most people, it will.

We like to tick the box indicating that $3 goes to the Presidential Election Campaign. While it is not abundantly clear to us that this has an impact, the general idea is that candidates that accept money from this fund are swearing off private donations. It is a hope, more so than an effective tool to keep private money out of politics. This is also pretty much the only time that you can directly choose where your tax dollars go. Ironically, this makes it the least democratic and most anti-societal thing you can do on this form.

If you have children, you can put them in as dependents. If you aren't sure if you have any children, let's just skip over this section, because the questions get rather sensitive rather quickly.

That was easy, wasn't it? Take a deep breath if you like, but if you're fired up and ready to go, full steam ahead!

Income

There are two types of income, and we tax them differently. There's earned income (that would be from your job). You're going to get a W-2 on that. If you have a business, there may be a business tax return. If you've done any contract work for someone and you've made over $625, they are required to send you a 1099.

That earned income is taxed at your income tax bracket. What will that be? That depends on all of your household income. It depends on the number of dependents you have and the number of deductions. That's on the next page of the tax form.

The other type of income is investment income. You may get something called a 1099B if you have interest on bank accounts or bonds, or if you get stock dividends or capital gains (meaning you sold something for more than you paid for it). You'll have that showing up on a 1099B.

Investment income is taxed differently than earned income. The interest from those bank accounts or bonds will be taxed at your income tax rate, but the capital gains and dividends are taxed at a lower rate. The tax laws will change many times throughout your lifetime, so pay attention. Make sure you know what your politician is considering voting "yes" on and how it will affect your pocketbook.

Those W-2s and those 1099s are also reported to the IRS, and the IRS matches those forms with our returns. They're a little slow, but they will catch up with you. They may send you a notice saying you missed something from a couple of years back.

The Big Question Is: What Isn't Taxed?

Investment income that is in a retirement account isn't taxed. Many times, we will have people call and say: I haven't gotten my 1099B on my retirement account. Well, you won't get one on a retirement account. (If you withdraw funds from a retirement account, you will receive a 1099R.) If you take qualified withdrawals from Roth IRAs, those withdrawals are tax exempt. If you have business losses, you won't pay tax on the loss; you may get a tax advantage there.

When we tell people that all there is to doing your taxes is walking down the 1040, the following is a pretty good illustration of that.

Read the first line (line 7): Wages, salaries and tips. Attach forms W-2. If you received any W-2s from any employers, this is where that information goes. Easy. They're just asking how much you made.

Interest and dividends (lines 8a - 9b) and capital gains (line 13) make up the investment income. Self-employment income will go in line 12. Most of this stuff is fairly self-explanatory—if you own a farm you will put income from that on line 18, for instance. This is where IRA income, pensions, rental property, Social Security benefits and more get reported.

Let's take a closer look at line 13. This will be relevant if you have investments in taxable accounts. One of the great things about capital gains is that you get to control when you realize them, and losses can offset gains. You only pay taxes on the gains (difference between sale price and purchase price of the security). You can report more detailed information about these gains on Schedule D. Keeping track of your cost basis is very important. Before 2011, brokerages were not required to keep track of this vital information, so tracking it down for older investments can sometimes be a huge, time consuming hassle. The next time you hear someone gripe about millennials, remind them that at least nobody will have to waste their time tracking down their cost basis information.

If you get to line 22 and know that you haven't put some source of income down, go back and figure out where it goes. Otherwise, add everything up and pat yourself on the back.

Not so hard, huh? Recline a little more in your seat and take a well-deserved deep breath and a bite of chocolate.

Now that you have your TOTAL INCOME, it's time to adjust it.

Adjusted Gross Income

This is where you start reducing your income for tax purposes. You will end this section with an Adjusted Gross Income, or AGI. This is the basis for figuring out your taxes owed, but let's not get ahead of ourselves. Just go line by line and see if you can reduce your income with these common expenses.

Line 23 gives teachers the opportunity to deduct $250 of unreimbursed classroom expenses. Why do teachers get their own line here? We hardly pay them anything, they work long hours while being expressly exempt from overtime protections, we treat them as a punchline in a classic dumb joke about inability, and we berate them for our children's shortcomings. They raised and shaped every one of us and are the most vital defenders of the future of our nation. Knocking a couple of dollars off of their taxes is quite literally the least we can do. If you want to take it a step further, buy a teacher some classroom supplies or happy hour drinks.

If you contributed to a Health Savings Account or a personal retirement account, this is where you put that information. If you are making less than $80,000 ($160,000 if married filing jointly) and are paying interest on student loans, you can deduct up to $2,500 of it here. Again, just take this section step by step and add everything up on line 36. Subtract that from your TOTAL INCOME on line 22, and you have arrived at your AGI.

Time for another deep breath and another bite of chocolate. Maybe take this opportunity to stretch your legs, get some fresh air, or call your senator about a pressing issue.

We have now made it to page 2.

Tax and Credits

This is a little misleading. The bulk of this section is more deductions and credits. A deduction reduces your income, but a credit reduces your taxes. Similar concept, just different calculations. But deductions and tax credits of the same dollar amount don't amount to the same savings. Tax credits are far more valuable, dollar for dollar.

And don't forget those IRA contributions on line 32. Those are also due by the tax filing deadline (usually April 15th). The annual limit varies depending on the year, so check the limit. See the section below on cutting taxes for why this is important.

Line 38 is like the free square in Bingo - just write whatever you wrote on Line 37 to bring it to the back page. Fun, easy, relaxing.

If Line 39a is relevant to you, then you are either over 65 or blind, and you get a higher deduction than the standard. The handy explainer next to line 40 directs you to the instructions again, as do we. Most people will get the standard deduction, so just write that one on line 40. If you had large medical expenses, mortgage interest payments, charitable contributions, taxes paid (not including federal taxes) or a few other miscellaneous expenses, you may benefit from itemizing expenses. Check out Schedule A for more information. If these expenses add up to more than your standard deduction, itemize and send in the Schedule A along with your 1040.

41 is an easy math problem, and 42 is also a fairly easy math problem on exemptions. Actually calculating your taxes is the trick of this whole sheet. If your income is simple and only came from one or a few sources, you can probably use the tax table in the instructions. You simply put your finger on the number closest to your income, look slightly to the right of your finger and put this number down on line 44.

There are some credits on lines 48-54 that can directly reduce the amount of tax you owe. If any of these apply, add them up on line 55 and subtract that from line 47.

Don't take a break yet, the next section is still more of the same—you're in the groove; keep it rolling.

Other Taxes

See if any of these apply to you. Critically, if you were self-employed, this is where most of your taxes will come into play. You can see here that you should put that stuff on schedule SE to calculate tax owed there. There are some extra taxes that you might have owed here, too.

Add everything up on line 63, and then have a BIG sigh. You just coast from here.

You've earned a drink. Pour yourself a glass of water, and stretch your back muscles out.

Payments

Payments should be fairly self-explanatory. If you have paid taxes already or taxes have been paid on your behalf, you note that here. You will probably have this information on your W-2 or 1099s from work. There are a few last credits shoved in as well. Check this for all that you have already paid or might be owed back.

Add this all up on line 74 and queue up a drumroll in your head for the big reveal.

Refund or Amount You Owe

Line 75 has a revealing question for you. If you have been paying taxes all year (through quarterly payments or withholdings), this is where you find out if you were paying the right amount. Basically, there is a number which is the taxes you owe on all of that income and a number which you have already paid. If you owe more than you have already paid, you will move down to line 78; if you have paid more than you owe, you get to tell the IRS where to send your money.

The best way to get your refund is direct deposit. If you would rather split your refund up amongst several accounts or buy a savings bond instead (weirdo), you can do that with Form 8888.

Don't bother with line 77; you can pay those taxes when you get there.

If you owe taxes, pull out your checkbook or check out the fairly straightforward instructions on how to pay by phone or online.

Sign and date the form, write in your occupation and exhale.

See! That wasn't so hard.

In any of this, the hard part is gathering all of your information. The advantage that we have now is much of that information is available digitally—you can find it online. W-2s must be sent out by the end of January, and by the middle of February you should be receiving 1099s. The 1099s have your dividends and your interest, along with any contract labor. If you had a retirement account, remember that you don't have to pay any taxes on the dividends or the capital gains in a retirement account. But, if you did take distributions from the retirement account, you'll get something called a 1099-R. You need to gather all of that paperwork— and, again, much of it is available online which makes it very easy—but you need to go back and look at your tax returns from last year. What's the same? What has changed? Do you have different income sources? With those W-2s…do you have more than one job? Make sure you get all of the paperwork together to get ready to file your taxes.

Then, watch out for those other deductions if you do file that report. You may track them in a notebook. Keep your receipts. (You can pop them in a shoebox.) With smartphones, a great thing to do is just snap pictures on your phone of those receipts (remember to back up your phone so these aren't lost!) or take a note as you go along to track all of those items to make it easier. That's the real secret with your taxes. If you keep up with the paperwork all along, it's very simple.

You don't need to keep all of your receipts for every item you purchase during the year. If you have a business or a business on the side, you need to track all of the receipts related to that business. Also, if you make donations, you need to have verification of all those donations.

Doing taxes yourself by hand is a useful exercise in civics. If you are just starting out in your career, you will probably not have a hard time of it. The key is to be organized with your documents on the front end and to block out some quiet time to complete the paperwork. If that doesn't work, try an online tool or hire a professional.

Online programs will walk you through the process line by line, with explanations along the way. The software will even do the calculations for you! Many people are filing online now through e-file. We have many software packages that you can do your taxes through. Of course, you have to pay to use them unless you qualify for 'Free-File,' which is for families making below a certain level of income. Qualifiers can go to the IRS website and find a button for 'Free File' to see which service providers are available to them. If your income is above the limit, you may have to pay for access to the software, or you can get the paper forms. If you use printed forms, submit them the old-fashioned way with a stamp.

We also have other tax assistance available. Through the IRS there is a system called VITA (Volunteer Income Tax Assistance), which is volunteer tax assistance for families earning below a certain level of income. Go to the website and use the Locator Tool to find a location nearest to you (or phone 800-906-9887). There is also a Locator Tool to find an AARP Tax-Aide location close to you (or phone 888-227-7669). If you'd prefer, you may call 211, which is actually the United Way, and tell them your ZIP code. They will tell you the nearest office to get some assistance.

There are also many tax prep companies out there at this time of year. We prefer to go to our CPA (Certified Public Accountant). They are licensed and have to stay abreast of the rules and regulations. You want to make sure you take advantage of every deduction that's available, because, yes, we want to pay our taxes, but that doesn't mean we want to overpay our taxes.

If at the end of filing, you realize you owe taxes, you can pay electronically. We urge you not to pay by credit card, because it encourages us to let that credit build on our statements. There may be additional fees to use credit cards and debit cards, and the fees can be pretty steep. You can pay with a check, if you can actually find your checkbook (if you ever had one). As the way we transfer money changes, the IRS is working to keep pace. Cut them a little slack. It's the government.

The IRS has a smartphone app (IRS2Go). So if you've already filed, you can check on your refund status, you can get tax tips and even get some of your very own tax records through that app.

Our deadline to file taxes is usually April 15th. If you file an extension—and you can file one—it requires you to make a payment. You must send the form for the extension in along with the payment that you expect to make when you do eventually file your taxes.

If there's a mistake on your taxes, don't panic. Know that you can amend those returns. Go back and find the information you need to correct your previous tax mistakes or omissions. If someone helped you file those taxes, call them when the IRS notifies you and work together to get the job done.

If you miss reporting income, same thing. You're just going to go back and correct your omission. What often happens with capital gains, because of missing information, it may look as if there is no cost basis. This makes it look as though you owe a whole lot of money. Again, don't panic. Go back and look through old statements and records to find when you initially purchased a security.

It's highly unlikely that the IRS is trying to lock you up and throw away the key. They just want you to pay your fair share, and they understand that things can get missed along the way.

Refund

If you're going to get a tax refund, it's possible you're having too much deducted from your paycheck. Consider looking at your deductions and adjusting how much you're withholding in taxes with the appropriate person at your workplace (HR or Accounting).

Some people like receiving that tax refund every year, though, because it's a form of forced savings. Whether you get a refund each year or just every once in a while, the question you have to answer is: What are you going to do with that extra money? We're asking you to please not spend all of it. Yes, you can treat yourself a little bit, but let's consider some other options.

What Can You Do With an Extra Lump Sum of Money?

Consider paying down any credit card debt you've accumulated. That's a great use of that money! Get rid of those high interest charges. This is also an excellent opportunity to beef up your emergency savings account (or start one if you haven't already). And, how about this: save for a summer vacation. Summer's going to be here before you know it. If you have children, put some of it in education savings accounts. Years later, you're going to be glad you did. And, finally, think about adding it to your retirement. You can start an IRA now that will count on next year's taxes.

If you have to spend part of it, we suggest you go halves. Spend half of it on something fun, and invest or save half of it. That half can go a long way! Don't get to summer and have nothing to show for it. This is sort of like lagniappe. Treat it as such, but don't be foolish with it.

How Do You Cut Your Taxes?

We always tell people: Pay yourself rather than paying Uncle Sam. The best way to do that is to fund your retirement plan. Tax time is a good time to review your 401(k) and decide whether or not you're putting enough aside. If you're under 50, you can put $18,500 aside. That reduces your federal income tax bill. If you're 50 or older, you can set aside $24,500. Contribution limits do change over the years, so remember to check on the IRS website each year to see if you can contribute more.

If you want to help your bill for the past year, or what's going to be due on April 15th, contribute to a Traditional IRA. Remember, you have until April 15th, not December 31st, to make your contribution for the past year. There are income limits for making IRA contributions, so depending on how much income you or your spouse earn and how you file your taxes, you may or may not be eligible to contribute to an IRA. You can put $5,500 in an IRA if you're under 50, $6,500 if you're 50 or older; and each person can fund his or her own IRA account. So, if you're married, you and your spouse can both contribute the $5,500 (or $6,500 depending on age) to your respective accounts. Whatever you put in will reduce your income, which means it's going to lower your taxes. You don't pay taxes on the money you put into the IRA until you take that money out, and you only ever pay taxes on the original amount you put in—not the growth of the investments.

Another type of account you can contribute to is a Roth IRA. A Roth IRA is not going to give you a break on your tax bill, but it will help you later on. We have higher income limits for Roth IRAs than for Traditional IRAs, but the same contribution limits apply: $5,500 for under 50 and $6,500 for 50 or older. This doesn't reduce your current tax bill, but the future growth is never taxed. These limits can change from year to year, so check the IRS website.

Tax time is a prime opportunity to get started on an IRA for next year. Go ahead and open an account. Even if you can only do a small amount, $50 or $100 a month, it's worth it. Use a bank draft to automatically transfer your monthly contributions to your account. A little goes a long way.

Year-End Tax Planning

As the year draws to a close, we approach the end of our tax reporting year. This is a time to look at charitable giving and tax loss harvesting.

Charitable Giving

Charitable donations can include cash, securities and personal property. Most organizations will not put a value on your donated personal items. You must do that yourself. We tell people: Be reasonable. Don't overestimate an item's worth, because that could be a red flag for the IRS.

We also work with a lot of our clients to give away securities, such as stocks, bonds, mutual funds and exchange traded funds (ETFs). The value of the security on the day the charity receives it is the value of your donation. We look for the securities that have appreciated in value, because we want to give away that capital gain rather than realize it. Instead of selling the security and giving away the cash, we give away the security itself. This benefits both you and the charity, because you avoid paying tax on the gain and the charity gets the benefit of the growth of the security. This is only relevant in taxable accounts, because, as you remember, you don't pay taxes on the gains in retirement accounts.

Donations must be made by December 31st, but many custodians have earlier deadlines for distributions of cash or securities as charitable gifts. Check with your custodian to be certain you get your request in before the cutoff date.

Make sure you get a receipt, and make sure you're giving to a tax deductible organization (a qualified charitable organization). You can check the standing of a charitable organization with your Secretary of State, as well as see what percentage of funds received by the charity go to charitable projects. There are other websites available, such as CharityWatch.org that will provide this information as well.

Be wary of door-to-door, phone and email solicitations asking for donations. Don't commit to anything on the front-end. Ask for mailing information, and do the legwork to verify that you are giving to a charitable organization and that the person soliciting your donation is actually associated with that charity. You're not being rude; you're being responsible.

Tax Loss Harvesting

In taxable accounts, we look for any losses to harvest. This is a more difficult endeavor in years when the stock market performs well. You may want to harvest losses for a couple of reasons: to counter realized gains and/or to deduct the loss from your taxes. Remember to balance long term gains against long term losses, long term meaning you've held the security for a year or more. Each year, you may deduct up to $3,000 of realized losses (meaning you've actually sold the security) in taxable accounts, $1,500 if you're single or married filing separately.

Watch out for something called the wash rule. If you sell a loser, you can't buy it back for 31 days or else you lose that tax advantage.

If you have mutual funds, they are required to send out all of their dividends and capital gains before the end of the year. That can sometimes surprise people, because you never quite know how much that's going to be.

Odds and Ends

Take a look at your medical expenses. Remember, those deductibles start all over January 1st. Get in those annual check-ups before you head out to go shopping (and maybe before the holiday meal at Thanksgiving). Renew your prescriptions before the end of the year (if you can).

Look at any credit cards points, airline rewards and bonus items. Many of those rewards and points will expire at the end of the year. You don't want to miss out on any of those.

As a Wise P.I.G.G.Y. Once Said:

- Expect W-2s and 1099s from most sources by February of each year.

- Keep up with relevant receipts.

- Check out irs.gov to see if you qualify for tax prep assistance.

- Hire a CPA if you're having trouble.

- Adjust payroll deductions to fit your needs.

- Make a charitable donation or two to a legitimate organization.

- Pay your taxes. It's your civic duty!

Plan on not working.

What Does It Mean to Retire?

For the most part, it means exiting the workforce, or at least stepping out of your main career and into something less demanding, which generally translates into a job that pays less—much less or even nothing like volunteering.

We haven't been kicking around the idea of retirement for very long. It was only a few generations ago that such an idea was possible. Most people only stopped working when they died. They worked long and hard at physically-demanding jobs and stopped when their bodies could no longer carry the load. Lifespans were shorter back then, so the idea of the golden years was futuristic.

For those who kept on kicking, it was up to their families to support them. They and their children lived on the same patch of dirt, sometimes in the same house, and it was expected that older members would be cared for when the time came. But, life has changed drastically since then.

Longer lifespans mean that we're facing more time in retirement than in our working years. Think about working 30 years, then retiring at 55. If you live to 90, you are retired LONGER than you were in the workforce. Add in improving healthcare, and we are seeing the rise of people making it past 100. People just entering the workforce today should plan to live past 100. If you don't want to spend 80 of those 100 years toiling away at a job just to make ends meet, you need to start early on your retirement savings plan.

Aahhh...Retirement

A period of life when you can BYOB (be your own boss). No one controls your time but you. And probably that little dog you own from what we've seen. You can travel the country or hop around the globe. You can pen your memoir and if you find out it's boring, you can embellish it. Make it a fantasy and write fan fiction on what your life might've been like if you were secretly a spy. Remodel your house or downsize. Start your own business. Throw yourself into art. Spend your summers by the lake and your winters in the hot springs. Red hat society. Endless brunch. Netflix forever.

Maybe that's not your dream of retirement. Maybe yours is a little more noble. Finally have the time to volunteer. Mentor a child—not one related to you. Start a community garden. Adopt a stream. Honor a veteran. Become an advocate. Serve.

That's the dream. Of course, the dream usually leaves out some of reality, like the reality of healthcare costs. This is the biggest concern for people in those golden years. We may live longer, but we require more maintenance. Medicare and all its alphabet soup of parts is not totally free. And you'll need a supplemental policy if you don't want to fork over the cost of some medical expenses out of pocket.

What if you want to retire early? How are you going to pay for your health insurance premiums until you make it to the qualifying age for Medicare? Maybe now you realize you can't afford to retire until you qualify. Maybe you just need to write your congressman and start lobbying for Medicare for all!

There's still all the normal everyday expenses you'll need to cover in order to maintain your lifestyle—and your life. Food. Gas. Electricity. Replacing the washing machine. Car insurance. Taxes. Internet. Will you still have a mortgage in retirement? Will there be other debt you're dealing with? Do you want to travel? Will you be staying in Motel 6 or cruising on a luxury liner?

You're Young. Why Should You Think About Retirement Now?

So, you're not even 30, and you don't plan to retire anytime soon. Do you really need to start dreaming of retirement when you've barely started working on your career? YES! It's important to start imagining what life will be like when you quit your nine to five. That dream will change as you do, but you need to start thinking about it. Any delay may result in smaller dreams and fewer choices.

Whatever your dream of retirement may entail, know that it isn't free. If your dream includes being able to step away from a day in and day out job while still maintaining your lifestyle, well, you're going to need to start saving for it. Because, hear us when we say this: No one is saving that money for you.

Put your savings in the right places and invest it wisely, and you'll witness the beauty of compounding. Time will be one of your greatest allies. Pay attention to your investments, and you'll learn how connected we all are— how we all play a part in driving the economy. You'll be motivated to help it grow, because as the economy grows, so do your investments.

Start dreaming of retirement now, while you're just beginning to climb the ladder of success. Hold onto an idea of what life will be like when you stop working. Your dreams will keep you focused on that far away goal and keep you from sabotaging your future with impulse shopping and an expensive lifestyle.

How Much Do You Need to Save for Retirement?

Hopefully, we've convinced you that you shouldn't be spending your entire paycheck in the present and that you definitely shouldn't be living beyond your means. But you have to make it through to the end of the month. You have bills to pay, groceries to buy and a few vices to feed—a few present-day thrills aren't all bad.

How do you balance both saving for retirement and paying the bills? Maybe you aren't even making much money right now. It's likely you aren't if you're in your 20s. That's okay. Figure out how much you CAN save— yes, make a budget, see what's left over after your necessary expenses— and start there. What's feasible? (And don't forget to sock some away in an emergency fund for car repairs or future rent. You don't want to be in a situation where you tap into your retirement savings to pay off an unexpected expense. That's bad.)

Research says that we need to save 16.9% every year for THIRTY years if we want to keep the same lifestyle in retirement that we had while working. If you read 16.9% and can't imagine being able to put away that much right now, then, hey, relax. Breathe. Take a knee.

This number includes your contribution plus any match that may come from your employer. Still not enough? Don't throw up your hands in surrender. Do what you can right now. We're not all at the same places in our careers. But contribute something today. You don't want to wake up in a decade and realize you haven't put away anything, do you Rip Van Winkle?

A good rule of thumb when you take that first job is to sign up for a 10% contribution. Many employers will match 3 to 5%. You can see that will put you closer to 17%. It's your first real job. You've been making peanuts before, so taking 10% off the top before you get used to more income should be easy. You won't miss it! Socking away more money on the front-end of your career pays off more than waiting to start in your 40s. Remember compound interest!

By the time you hit your 40s, you will probably be at peak spending time—kids, house, new appliances, more cars, etc. If you've stowed away a lot at first, you can take a breather during this difficult period. That's not to give you permission to stop contributing! You just may have to pull back a little to cover bigger expenses.

Remember, this will be the money that pays for your lifestyle (and life) when you decide to step out of the daily grind of the workforce. You may have heard of it as paying yourself. That's a great way to look at it. You want to be your own boss in retirement. You want to answer to no one except for the call of the wild and your sidekick Charlemagne the miniature schnauzer. Well, your boss—you—needs a pool of money in order to have an employee—you—to support. When you're analyzing your budget and how much you can afford to save out of every paycheck, think about what you'll be putting that away for. Hint: it's you—the you that answers to no one.

If you are fortunate enough to work for a company that has benefits like a matching program in a 401(k) or an IRA, take full advantage of that match. If the company says they'll match 1% of your salary that you contribute, then AT LEAST put in that 1%. If they match 3%, put in 3%. 5%, put in 5%. 10%, put in 10%. If your company matches 3%, for example, then to make it to that 16.9% contribution target, all you have to contribute now is 14%.

The company match is NOT the most you can put towards retirement. It's the starting point for your contribution. If the company match is 3%, and you put in 3%, you just earned 100% on your money. What a deal! But don't stop there. The annual contribution limit is a dollar amount that is set by the IRS each year.

Does the match where you work increase every year you work there? You're going to want to check so that you can increase the amount you're contributing. If you are just starting out and can't afford to contribute more than the match, that's fine. Go back and examine your budget each year. Can you contribute more this year? Did you get a raise? Don't spend that raise; increase your contribution to your retirement account! You don't have to contribute all of your raise, but split it. Half you pocket now, half you put away for your future.

Prioritizing your retirement savings now, in the present, will be an incredible reward for your future self. Future self will be so pleased. So look out for your future self. Make your future self proud.

Why is It Important for You to Think About Retirement Now?

It's a scary world out there for someone approaching retirement. Lay-offs and forced early retirement, corporate scandals and disappearing stock value, shrinking pension benefits, and, now, a Social Security system heading for hard times. What's a body to do?

The most valuable asset anyone can have is their ability to work and earn a living. For those who are already retired, the scariest thing is knowing there are no more paychecks to be had. Whatever you generate must come from assets you have built up through a lifetime of saving and investing. What if you didn't save enough? What if you picked the wrong investments? What if rising healthcare costs eat into your stash? What if inflation skyrockets and leaves your earnings in the dust?

In 1950, General Motors started the first pension plan for its employees. The idea was simple. GM would set aside a certain amount for each employee, investing it, and adding to it until the employee retired. Upon retirement, the employee would receive a monthly check from GM until his death. Company loyalty was rewarded with guaranteed payouts in old age.

Pensions—the old standard of the guaranteed payment every month when you retire after you've been working at a place for thirty years or so—are dying out. These are called defined benefit plans. Your retirement is defined by your benefit package—overall salary and how long you've worked there. With these plans, employees have little risk. Just show up and work. Keep showing up for a long time, and you get a monthly stipend in retirement that covers you until you die. Some state employees still have these, and some big utility companies still offer them, but they are fazing out for younger employees.

Shifting the Risk

Laws have changed, and employers found they didn't want the responsibility or the cost of dealing with these plans. More and more, companies have turned to defined contribution plans. 401(k)s, profit-sharing plans and 403(b)s are defined contribution plans. With these, the risk is all on you, the employee. If you don't put money into the plan, there is none to take out. If you don't choose the investments within the plan wisely, you will have less. If you don't monitor fees and demand good options, your account will suffer. Upon retirement, whatever has accumulated in your account is what you have to live on in your old age. This change has marked a shift in risk. In the old plans, the employer took all the risks. In the new plans, the employee takes all the risks.

For most people, they will have to accumulate enough in their defined contribution plans in order to create their own monthly stipend that will pay out until they die. And that's where it gets tricky! How much will you need each month? Will that amount change? What pile of money can produce that monthly paycheck? How long will you live? It requires each of us to be actuaries and investment pros in order to answer these questions.

When the employer was shouldering the risk, there was a need for some sort of protection, so the Pension Benefit Guaranty Corporation (PBGC) was created. This is a government agency, which acts as an insurance company on pension plans. Should a company go bankrupt, PBGC was supposed to step in to cover those guaranteed payments to employees. This seemed like a no lose proposition.

Then, times changed. The steel industry went through hard times, and, time and again, the Pension Benefit Guaranty Corporation was called on to fill the gap. Tough economic times combined with tough times in investment markets left many pension plans in a pickle. Although United States retirees will continue to receive a check thanks to PBGC, many are finding that check reduced considerably.

Some old line companies offer both types of plans (defined benefit and defined contribution), but newer companies only offer 401(k)s or profit-sharing plans (defined contribution). There are no guaranteed payouts, only an opportunity to save and invest at will. As scary as the situation is with the old pension plans, academics are concerned about employee behavior with the new plans. When those employees retire who only have a 401(k) and Social Security to depend on, will it be enough? Will those employees cry foul, saying they didn't know enough to handle the risk thrust upon them?

In studying employee behavior in these plans, research has found most people to be lacking in knowledge. The average contribution rate is only about 4%, a rate which will leave many in poverty at retirement. Also, most adopt a fund selection strategy called conditional naive diversification. No matter how many funds are offered within a plan, employees, on average, select three or four funds. That may not be so bad. Any more than that can be difficult to track, but most employees simply divide their contribution evenly among all chosen funds. If you select four funds, you tend to allocate 25% to each fund. Here's something interesting researchers have found... if you select only three funds, the math is not so easy (100% divided by three), so, instead employees put more in one fund, then divide the rest equally between the other two. So much for a reasonable allocation among cash, stocks and bonds based on time horizon and risks. Instead, people just split it up evenly and run with it.

We also know that few people change their original allocation. They rarely adjust to accommodate changing markets or their own aging. They're just not paying attention. Also, if company stock is offered within the plan, employees consider that separately. They don't even think of that in light of the allocation to other funds. Instead, they consider it as just something extra.

Enron and WorldCom employees know the danger of depending on company stock too heavily. Should the company disappear, your retirement goes down the tube. That may not be so horrible if you're 30 when it happens, but what do you do when it happens at age 50? Throw in the solvency problem with Social Security, and we're back to a scary world.

What Is Social Security?

One Defined Benefit plan that is still available to all of us is Social Security. Social Security has been around for over 80 years. Younger people laugh and assume it won't be there. While that's a good approach because it keeps you saving on your own, don't discount this program. At this point, we expect Social Security to replace about 40% of our pre-retirement income. That makes it an important component to our retirement and a good reason to keep in touch with your congressmen and congresswomen.

Some history first: It was modeled after Civil War pensions. Germany was the first country to enact a social insurance program in 1889. We passed our law in August of 1935 under President Franklin Delano Roosevelt, and it was a response to the Great Depression. Many people were aging and had no income.

When Social Security was first enacted, the tax was at 1% and worked its way up to 3% by 1948. We've always had a system where contributions to the plan are split between employee and employer. Right now, 6.2% comes out of your paycheck for Social Security, and your employer puts in another 6.2% for a total of 12.4%. This is part of the FICA tax. The other 1.45% that comes from your paycheck goes into Medicare. Your employer matches this, as well.

The first recipient was Ida May Fuller. She only paid in for 3 years for a total of $24.75. Her first check was almost that much at $22.54. Ida May outlived the actuary. She lived to be 100 years old and collected a total of $22,888.92—a great return.

We've had some amendments on Social Security. 1950 was the first time they introduced Cost of Living Adjustments (COLA), which are very important to Social Security recipients. At that time, Congress had to approve every single one of the adjustments, but in 1972 the COLAs became automatic (and that's been part of our problem).

1983 was the last time—more than 30 years—we had big changes. The country was experiencing financial problems. At that time, they increased both taxes and the retirement age. But it's been over 30 years; we need to look at these pieces again. In the year 2000, we had the removal of an earnings limit for those who have reached full retirement age, so recipients can still work.

Well, everyone says: Will the money last? Remember, this is a pay as you go system. The money you're putting in now is not sitting in an account for you. It's paying for people who are already drawing on Social Security. Our problem is that we have fewer workers per retiree. When the program began, there were seven workers for every retiree. We were able to accumulate extra money and store up for a rainy day. Well, now it's pouring! Our aging population and longer lifespans are putting a strain on the system.

Right now, we know that by 2033, we won't have enough to pay full benefits. We will still be paying out those benefits, but only 77 cents on the dollar (if we do nothing to change the program). So, it's time for another amendment. Here are some options. We can increase the annual earnings to be taxed. Right now, if you make over $118,000, you'll see that tax drop off. We can increase the Social Security tax, now at 6.2%. We can increase the retiree age, which is what we did the last time changes were being made. And we may see some changes to the Cost of Living Adjustments.

Social Security is an important income component in retirement, and you should want the program to be healthy and available when it's your turn to draw on it. That's why you need to vote! Get involved and pay attention. And run for office! If you don't participate in the national conversation, all you'll be left with is a defined contribution plan that may or may not be enough.

If Social Security covers 40% of retirement income, the other 60% has to come from our savings. We need to be able to replace—between Social Security and that 401(k)—about 85% of our pre-retirement income if we want to live a decent life. What we're finding, though, is that we're not saving enough.

What Does All This Mean?

The first thing we have to do is: We MUST increase our contributions to retirement savings. We point to what's happening with state employees here in Mississippi. Right now, between what the employees are putting in and what the state is putting in, the total retirement contribution is now a little over 22%. That needs to be our guideline. We need to be aiming for setting aside 20-25% of our money, between employee and employer matches, for retirement.

We also need to get help with the investment choices. Most of the time, you're given a set of mutual funds or exchange traded funds to choose between. If you're not sure how to choose which funds to invest in, find someone you can pay by the hour once a year to look at your options with you. Get educated about those funds and make appropriate choices.

We have to face the hard fact that we may have to work longer. We may have to delay our retirements in order to build up the amount that we need saved. For many people, they're going to be facing part-time work even in retirement.

The good news for younger people is that time is on your side. Go ahead and start increasing your contributions, looking at your set of investment choices and making the most of the time you have right now. It's easier when you're 30 than when you're 50.

The best thing to do is to follow the old adage: Don't put all your eggs in one basket. Don't give up on a pension plan if you happen to have one, but invest outside of it, as well. Invest in your company 401(k), and do it wisely. If you need help, find an advisor. Give your plan an annual check-up to make sure it's doing what you want it to do. Don't load up on company stock. Invest outside of retirement plans, too. Add to regular savings on a disciplined basis. Save and invest like you'll never draw another paycheck. One day, that will be the case.

And last, but not least... don't factor in Social Security. Think of it as icing on the cake. If it doesn't come through, you won't go hungry.

Where Do You Put Retirement Savings?

All right. You're on board. You've decided to commit and get on the retirement savings bandwagon. Excellent! You're going to learn to cook and eat leftovers, get a library card, realize you don't need another new phone, host Mario Cart parties at your house and maybe even take up running. Maybe just easy walking to podcasts. No pressure. So where do you put this money that you've decided not to spend on extra dinners and clothes and gadgets and books and coffees and pub nights and whatever you're overspending on?

There are three types of accounts you can put your money in. Why three types? Taxes. Everything is taxes.

Tax-Deferred Accounts (Traditional IRAs, 401(k)s, 403(b)s, There Are More...)

This is where you put your before-tax money. It goes right in, no taxes taken out. (We have to put in a qualifier here. No income tax is taken out, but you'll still see Social Security and Medicare taxes coming out.) This means that if you put a dollar into your tax-deferred account, it's not a dollar less on your paycheck; it may be 70 cents less. And the higher your tax bracket, the more sense it makes to save this way.

Tax-deferred means a delay in the taxes that are due. That delay also applies to the earnings in the account. The result is the account grows tax-free: no tax on interest, dividends or capital gains. You don't even have to keep up with the growth for filing purposes.

Remember, it's tax-deferred, not tax-free. You put the money in and invest it, and you can buy and sell securities and pay absolutely nothing on the earnings… for now. The government's intent is to eventually collect tax on this money, and that collection happens when you start withdrawing money from the account.

Because the government wants us to save for retirement and not be a burden on the State, they put in rules about when you can withdraw your money. These rules vary depending on the type of tax-deferred account, but most have a minimum withdrawal age of 59 and a half.

If you withdraw before that half birthday, there is a 10% penalty. Also, when you withdraw money, the tax will finally come due, and how much you pay in taxes will depend on your income tax bracket. That means withdrawing before 59 and a half may result in a tax and penalty of about a third of the amount—a hefty price tag! So, don't do that if you can help it.

With all the penalties and taxes, you might ask: Is this worth it? After all, what if you need that money before you're old enough to withdraw it penalty-free? Well, Congress built in a few exceptions to the penalty to encourage young people to keep tucking money away. One is the first-time purchase of a house up to $10,000. Another is to cover college expenses. And yet another is to cover big medical bills. Visit the IRS website for a complete list of exceptions.

So, yes, keep contributing to those tax-deferred accounts. You'll be saving money now for your future self. You'll be cutting your tax bill in the present, and you have a few outs in case you need to use the money for an immediate need.

Eventually, Uncle Sam wants his money. Again, it's tax-deferred, not tax-free. Once you reach a certain age—right now it's 70 and a half (again with the half)—you are required to start withdrawing a percentage of your retirement savings out of these accounts, which means you have to pay income taxes on the money you withdraw. No, you no longer have to worry about that 10% penalty, but you have to calculate income taxes on the withdrawals. The idea is that most people will be in a lower tax bracket in retirement, so the bill will be less when all is said and done.

The numbers and letters for each type of retirement account relate to a particular law or section of the IRS tax code. Think "paragraph 401(k)" or "403(b)." Each type has a different set of regulations, meaning differing contribution limits and differing guidelines upon retiring. Congress can update or change the rules, so make sure you pay attention!

This brings us to the next type of account, which doesn't require you to pay income taxes on the withdrawals. What? You heard us. No tax.

Tax Exempt Accounts (Roths)

Roth IRAs became the law of the land in 1997. Thank you, Senator Bob Packwood and Senator William Roth. They came up with this idea in 1989 and decided the Packwood IRA didn't have a ring to it. This type of account is quite a gift for retirement savers, especially if you have a long time until the big day.

You won't cut your tax bill NOW with contributions to a Roth IRA, but this tax break is for your future self. The contributions to your Roth IRA are taxed in the present. Why would you do this? Because the growth on the account is never taxed. NEVER. That means when you withdraw from the account in retirement, there is absolutely NO tax to pay. You've already paid tax on the original contribution. You don't pay tax on earnings. So, NO tax!

And, that's why these accounts are such a gift. The longer you have until retirement, the more earnings/growth you'll hopefully have on the account, resulting in a bigger tax break. The ability to take money out of this account without a tax bill means you'll be able to live almost tax-free in retirement. This way, if you find you still need or want extra money out of your retirement savings, but you don't want to pay more in income taxes by withdrawing excess funds from your tax-deferred retirement account, you can instead take it out of your Roth. Amazing.

If you're just starting out with lower income and lower income taxes, Roth IRAs are the way to go. Or, shall we say, one way to go? You don't need a tax break now, when you're in a lower income tax bracket, as much as you'll need one later. Remember, that is what this type of account does for you.

Another great thing about Roth IRAs is that there is no requirement to withdraw money when you reach 70 and a half. They offer more flexibility and can allow you to pass on money to your heirs more easily.

Finally, even though the Roth IRA also has that 59 and a half withdrawal penalty rule, the penalty only applies to earnings. Yes, you get the same exceptions as mentioned earlier with tax-deferred accounts, but more than that, you always have access to your original contributions. Remember, you've already paid tax on that money when you put it into the account, so taking it out (without withdrawing earnings) results in no penalty and no tax.

Taxable Accounts

The third type of account is a taxable account. Your money doesn't get to go in tax-free, and it doesn't get to grow tax-free. You pay tax on the capital gains and interest/dividends. It does allow withdrawals without tax consequences, though. It's your money, just waiting in the wings. You pay taxes on the realized capital gains—realized just means that you've actually sold that investment so it can't still go up or down with the stock market. You pay taxes on the dividends—some investments pay out dividends, which is a portion of their earnings. But the amount you pay in taxes for these has a cap of 15% for those earning less than $400k. Even if you're earning more than $400k a year, it's still less in taxes than your income-tax bracket, so, this is yet another great place to save your money.

Let's Back Up. What is a 401(k)?

It just happened to be the end of 2013 when Ryder was riding bikes around town with one of his friends. She was heading to graduate school after living and working in Jackson for a couple of years. He was being the nosy finance nerd and pestering her with questions about her student loans, current salary, expected salary range and her past job benefits. (Being a helpful and caring friend, he was also giving her his best advice on these matters too!) The old job had a 401(k) plan with a generous match, and he was relieved to hear that she had been contributing at least enough to get the full employer contribution. She knew that it was important to save for retirement and knew to take advantage of the benefit.

"Yeah, the stock market scares me, though, so I have it in what they said was the safest option. I think it is called a money market."

Cash.

She had her whole 401(k) in cash in a stretch of time when the S&P 500 returned over 50%! Even a moderate, can't go wrong, balanced fund returned 14% in 2012 and 21% in 2013! If she had invested her money, her $200/month savings could have grown to over $6,000 instead of being just $4,800. This would have been an amazing return for such a short time.

This just happened to be a time with particularly high returns. Other stretches of time and other investments would produce different returns.

Retirement is the biggest financial decision most people will make. In recent history, employers have typically provided some sort of mechanism for people to have income or assets after they finish their careers. With people living longer and longer these days, employer sponsored retirement plans have become more and more important.

The defined contribution plans put all the risk on the employee. YOU decide how much to put in the plan, and YOU decide which investments are appropriate for your savings. This means that it's of paramount importance for everybody—whatever your station in life, whatever your educational background—to learn about investing and about financial markets, so that you can make informed choices, because it's all on us now.

Every single 401(k)—or it may be called a 403(b) or something else (there are different numbers or names for these accounts)—has a separate legal document that defines how the plan will work. These plans are under a federal law called ERISA (Employment Retirement Income Security Act), which requires certain basic protections. However, each plan is different. It is a contract, and so you have to go to that plan's contract to find out:

- Is there a company match?

- How long before that match is all yours?

- How much can you contribute to the account?

- Who will be managing the plan?

- How do you make changes to contributions or investments?

- How often can you make these changes?

All of this information will be in this separate document. The actual plan can be quite lengthy, but you will usually get a copy of something called the "Summary Plan Description" with most of the answers to the above questions.

Essentially, your 401(k) works like this:

1. You decide an amount of money that you want withheld from your paycheck. Sometimes you can choose if you want this deferred before you pay taxes on it or after.

2. This money is then withheld and placed in an account for you.

3. Your employer may or may not add a contribution on top of this. Typically, contributions are matching contributions up to some percentage of your pay but can also include flat contributions or profit sharing contributions.

4. The money in the account is invested according to your instructions.

5. Money accumulates as you work and is invested as you instructed.

6. When you retire, you have essentially free access to the money.

If you deferred the income before you paid tax on it, then when you withdraw it in retirement, you will owe taxes on it as you would on income. If you did post-tax contributions, also known as Roth contributions, you will never owe taxes on it again.

There are also some limits to the amount of income that you defer into your 401(k) each year. For 2018, you can defer up to $18,500. That's a lot, but you can never contribute more than your income. These limits may change from year to year, so if you're looking to max out your contributions, check with your Human Resources department or with the IRS about your limits.

There are some key considerations to make when starting with a new 401(k). Also, for the record, there are a bunch of different names to retirement plans at work; we will just use the term 401(k) liberally and generically to cover defined contribution plans. These may include Roth 401(k)s, the TSP, SIMPLE IRAs, 457(b)s or 403(b)s or others.

Remember, it's all up to you! The two things you must decide are:

1. How much should you contribute?

2. How do you invest your 401(k) money?

So let's get started on some answers!

How Much Should You Contribute to Your 401(k)?

As much as you can! That's the short answer.

When you're interviewing for a job, you need to ask the question: Do you have a retirement plan? If so, how does it work? In some cases, you may not be able to sign up at the very beginning of your job; there may be a delay. If you can sign up immediately, be sure to do it first thing.

401(k)s have contribution limits. While most people never even get near those maximums, that should be your goal. As we mentioned earlier, the current maximum contribution for someone under the age of 50 is $18,500. This may seem like a lofty goal if you're only making $40,000 per year. Keep in mind that you have to start somewhere. We tell people to sign up to contribute at least 10%. Since this is salary deferral, remember that no income tax is taken out of these contributions.

Know that you can never contribute more than you earn. If your job is part-time but you can contribute to your employer plan, you will be limited by your total income. So, even though the annual maximum is now $18,500, if you're only making $12,000, then you can only contribute $12,000.

If 17% or even 10% sounds too steep for you right now, here's how to get started: Take advantage of any matching contributions your employer makes. It's common for employers to make a matching contribution of some sort to your retirement plan. This can take many shapes, but it's generally a match of up to a certain percentage of your income. If the company says they offer a 3% match, that means that if you defer 3% of your income, they will contribute another 3% on top, for a total of 6%. That's a 100% return on your money guaranteed. Can't beat that! But if you defer 4% or more, the company will still only match 3%, for a combined contribution of 7%. Don't let that stop you from going above and beyond, though. Remember, this is your retirement, and it's all on you. Also, if you defer less than the match, they will match your lower contribution. In other words, you've left money on the table.

So, take advantage of the employer match. At the very LEAST.

Next, you need to save more tomorrow. Every time you get a raise, defer a little bit more into your 401(k). If you get a 2% raise, split the gain— increase your contribution 1%. Even if you didn't get a raise, look at your budget annually and see if you can afford to raise your contribution. One feature that a lot of plans are starting to offer is that they will raise your contribution for you automatically every year. Automation in the 401(k) industry is an excellent behavioral tool for saving that you should take advantage of. Check to make sure that you are on the right track!

Not every plan does this, of course, so don't just assume that your contributions are increasing. Be diligent. Make sure you're increasing your retirement contributions over the years.

Target deferring 17% of your income, but don't hesitate to keep climbing.

Once you've worked your way up to the target of 17%, you can start aiming higher. The more aggressive you get with saving, the earlier you can retire. Early retirement is the dream, right? We ran the numbers, and if you save 20% of your income, 35 years of work should support a comfortable retirement. Saving 33% will bring that down to 25 years of work. If you save 50% of your income, you only have to work about 16 years to retire with enough money to cover your expenses! These numbers are very loose, obviously, as there are other factors to take into consideration, such as exactly how much you plan on spending in retirement. The general idea is that if you save more, you can meet your financial goals faster.

All that being said, the percentage to save is independent of the vehicle you save it in. If your 401(k) is not actually that good, it may make sense to put your money in a personal IRA or in a taxable account for the same purpose. But start first with that 401(k). Even if the fund choices aren't great or the fees are high, the ability to defer contributions through your paycheck along with employer matches usually makes it worth your while.

Now to question 2…

How Do You Invest Your 401(k) Money?

For many, investing in a 401(k) is their first experience with the world of investments, and it's usually overwhelming. It doesn't matter how smart you are or how educated you are, when they hand you that packet of information and the list of fund choices, your eyes will likely glaze over. Don't feel bad. Know that you CAN figure it out. With some knowledge of the language of investing and an understanding of how it all works, you can probably set up your retirement plan like a pro. If you need help, though, it's worth it to hire a professional to give you some guidance. That little bit of money on the front-end can pay huge dividends later in retirement.

The list of funds for your 401(k) is called a plan menu. This menu should be like those you encounter at the diner—something for everyone. If stocks scare you to death, you'll be able to choose that basic cash or savings account (but, seriously, seek professional guidance before you make that choice). If you're all about high-flying stocks, you'll be able to choose an aggressive fund that fits your needs. And there will be all kinds of options in between. Remember, though, this is not a time to make reckless choices.

Before you can choose your "meal," you need to know about the ingredients, the recipes and the costs. First up is to understand what a "pooled" fund is. It's the recipe.

A pooled fund is a portfolio or a collection of investments. These pooled funds are called mutual funds or exchange traded funds and are designed for retirement plans. Because they contain more than one investment, you get instant diversification and, hopefully, lower risk. The manager of the fund decides what will be in the portfolio, and, of course, you have to pay the manager for doing this work.

In order to decide which portfolio or pool is right for you, you need to understand a little about the ingredients. Securities are investments that are formally traded on an exchange, and they are just claims against an asset. There are two types of claims: equity claims and debt claims. Every security is either an equity claim or a debt claim or some combination of the two. Simple, right?

Equity means ownership. A stock is an equity claim. When you own a share of stock, you are an owner of the company. As an owner, you are entitled to a share of the company's earnings. If the company does well— sells a lot of stuff and manages their finances well—you make money. If they don't, you lose. That's part of being an owner of a business. You are dependent on other people (namely CEOs) to run the business for you.

Debt is self-explanatory. When you buy a debt claim, you are a lender. Someone or something is borrowing money from you. Bonds are debt claims. A couple of key considerations when loaning someone money are: Can they make the regular payments? Can they eventually pay you back? Bonds usually have regular schedules of payments, making their cash flow stream a bit more reliable than stocks, but they still represent risk. What if the company goes bankrupt?

Of course, there are other ingredients. Cash is just cash. Money market funds are simply portfolios of short-term cash instruments. They function like savings accounts, with a stable amount and small interest payments each month—little risk but little reward.

You may have heard of the trade-off between risk and reward. The basic idea is that higher returning investments are more volatile in the short run. So, while stock investments may give you 8% returns over ten or more years, they do have the risk of significant loss in any given month or year. Bonds, on the other hand, may only promise to return 3%, but won't fluctuate in value quite so much from month to month or year to year. And savings accounts right now? 1-2% if you're lucky!

You may also see funds that invest in real estate or commodities (like oil or gold). Sometimes, the plan menu will offer some of these odd ingredients, but, mostly, it's some version of cash, stocks or bonds. Knowing this will give you some direction in choosing the right funds for your retirement.

Back to the recipe…

If I see "steak tartare" on the menu, I know I'm going to get raw beef. If I see "mashed potatoes," I know it will be all potatoes, with a little milk and butter (okay, a lot of milk and butter), but no meat in this recipe. If I see "lasagna," I'm going to get a combination of things—pasta, meat, tomato sauce, and maybe a few other things thrown in. Well, the names on your 401(k) plan menu offer clues as to their ingredients. Like the diner, you can sometimes get surprised by what is served up, but the name is a good starting place.

Some hints?

Often, stock funds will have the word "stock" or "equity" in the name. "Cap" stands for capitalization and indicates the size of the company in the portfolio. Large-cap means big companies. Mid-cap is for medium-sized companies, and small-cap is for (wait for it) small companies. Sometimes the philosophy of the fund manager is indicated by "growth" or "value." Growth funds tend to invest in faster growth companies and can be more aggressive choices versus those of value funds.

You may invest in US stock funds or funds that invest in companies outside our borders. International or foreign funds invest in stocks that are NOT those of US companies. Global funds invest in US stocks and stocks of other companies; borders mean nothing to the manager.

Fixed-income in the name means you have a bond fund. Often, these have additional qualifiers related to maturity of the bonds such as short-term, intermediate-term or long-term. They may invest in "corporate" bonds or "government" bonds.

A name isn't everything, but it's a starting point. From there, you need to investigate every option on the menu to decide what is right for you. Below is a guide to that menu:

- **Stable Value** or **Money Market funds**. These are basically cash.

- **Fixed Income**. These are funds with bonds of various types. They may contain US Government Treasury bonds or corporate bonds, but the idea is that they will all pay interest to you at a supposedly reliable pace.

- **Stocks**. These may be divided up into US or International funds, or they may be divided by size and shape. Stocks are shares of companies. The value fluctuates with the successes and failures of the company. Funds can be either actively managed by someone trying to pick the companies with the best future, or they can be a passively managed index fund, just keeping track of a basket of stocks without much interference or cost.

- **Balanced Funds**. A mix of the other types of funds. These are all-purpose funds that contain ALL the ingredients. Think turkey pot pie.

- **Target Date/Life Cycle funds**. These are a special flavor of balanced fund that adjusts as you age. They typically have a retirement year in the name. They start off with aggressive, risky investments in stocks to drive return when you have a long time to grow, and then they get more conservative, moving to bonds and cash as you retire. They're a real "set it and forget it" type of fund.

A 2006 law allowed employers to use Life Cycle Funds as the default option. This is because researchers have found that people would sign up for a retirement plan, or the company would automatically sign them up, and then the employee would never choose the investments in the plan. So the employees' funds would be sitting there—for example a 25 year old's funds would be sitting in the account, not invested, earning now less than 1% and costing the employee in the long run. Not good! So, the default became Life Cycle Funds.

These target retirement funds or life cycle funds are based on our ages and the target date is when we think we're going to retire. Typically, there is one for every 5 years or every 10 years. Pick the one that is the closest match to your projected retirement date. The beauty of these funds is that they automatically adjust. They start out being more aggressive with more exposure to the stock market for younger employees. As you age, they automatically adjust to weigh more on the bonds or the fixed income side to get you ready for retirement when you'll start to draw on that money.

Target Date Funds are usually an acceptable default option. Just pick one that matches up with when you think you will retire and call it a day. When it comes to the target funds or even the balanced funds, remember, these are one stop mutual funds. Most people think they need to choose 3 to 4 mutual funds for their 401(k), and they randomly choose a set that has no rhyme or reason. If you choose a target/life cycle fund or a balanced fund, you likely don't need to choose ANY other fund. You have complete diversification with stocks, bonds, cash and real estate all in one convenient investment. There is no need to choose another fund. Don't even get tempted! Put down the pencil. Walk away from the keyboard. You're good.

If you have a little more experience or are working with an advisor, you might want to assemble your own portfolio of low cost index funds that are appropriate for the long term nature of the 401(k). Generally speaking, the more time you have before you need the money, the more aggressive or risky your investments can be. The closer you are to retirement, the higher proportion of bonds and cash you want in your portfolio.

If you're just starting out in a job and you have a long time until retirement, don't be afraid to be a little more aggressive. It's going to take a while before you have much in your account, so this is a good time to choose one good equity fund and throw it all in. Time will even out the ups and downs in the market, and you'll have the advantage of buying shares with each new paycheck. If the market corrects, good for you! You're buying shares at a lower price.

The trustees of your plan get to make all the decisions about the plan: who will manage the plan, who the administrator will be, which funds will be in the plan menu, how much everything will cost…but the risk is all in the hands of the employee (you). You're stuck with whatever your employer offers, which means you need to look carefully at those choices. You also need to consider all expenses related to the plan. Most plan fees are paid by the participants—that's you—versus the employer, so know what you are paying for.

Hopefully, the plan trustees/sponsors have done their best to get the lowest cost alternatives out there, because there are going to be administrative fees. There will be fees within each of the funds offered. Sometimes we may see the same exact fund in four or five different plans, but the costs are drastically different because of all these other layers of expenses and because the trustees didn't negotiate as well as they should have or didn't have as big of a plan to be able to negotiate as well in the first place. This difference in fees can have a drastic difference in how much you can accumulate in your account.

Consider opting for index funds. These are funds whose portfolio matches an index. We call them imitator funds. For instance, a fund that tracks the S&P 500 will be comprised of a portfolio of all 500 of the companies that are in the S&P 500. (Actually, it's more than 500, but that's a story for another day.) Index funds should have lower expense ratios and are excellent ways to participate in the market.

If the same funds are available to the general public, find out how those annual expenses compare to those available in your plan. What about administrative fees? Are there other fees or penalties attached to your account? If you compare and find your fees are higher than average, talk to your employer. Ask that they consider a change in provider. After all, many employers are also participants in the plan. It's important for everyone to get the best deal possible.

What if You Change Jobs?

If you leave your employer, you will no longer be able to contribute to that 401(k). Each 401(k) is tied to both the individual and the company. You have a few options once you move on, and this is where vesting comes into play.

Vesting is about ownership. It only applies to the employer match. Any money that you take out of your paycheck and put into a plan is yours the minute you put it in there. However, that employer match may have a vesting schedule attached to it that says after you've worked at the company for a year you can get 20% of the match and you must work up to five years before you get the full match. This is one strategy employers use to hang on to employees, because, of course, it's costly for them to hire and train new employees. The company has invested money in you through training, and, in return, they expect you to invest time in the company.

If you have a 401(k) with a new employer, you may be able to roll your old 401(k) into it. This makes sense if your new plan has good, low cost investments that are the best for your situation. Ask HR the question: Can

I rollover my old 401(k) to my new 401(k)? It depends on that plan's contract as to whether or not this is permitted. If you can, there's probably going to be paperwork that will take care of this.

As this is rarely the case, often the best option is to roll your 401(k) into a personal IRA. You can put it with a mutual fund, a bank or a discount broker, for instance—anywhere you want to. You can roll it over to an account that has your name with IRA (Individual Retirement Account), and then you can choose the investments within that account.

The worst thing you can do is take all of your money out and spend it. Even if you don't spend it, you will owe income tax and possibly an early withdrawal penalty of 10%. Don't do this. Also, if you take the cash out, your employer is required to withhold 20% and pay in for taxes on the assumption you WILL spend it. If you change your mind, you have to find that other 20% to put back or you'll face penalties and taxes. So, don't take possession of your 401(k) funds. Don't even cash a check made payable directly to you.

How Exactly Do You Rollover an IRA?

First things first. Open an IRA account with another institution—a brokerage account, a bank account, etc. Once you have an official account, complete the process with your old 401(k) provider. Give them your new account number and the name of the new custodian. This new custodian/broker/bank may have to sign paperwork agreeing to take that money and be responsible for it.

The result will be a rollover that is actually an institution to institution transfer. Even if a check shows up in your mailbox, it won't be made payable directly to you. It will be made payable to XYZ Bank for the benefit of Jane Doe. This avoids that 20% deduction for taxes and keeps your hands clean. No penalty. No taxes to pay at the end of the year.

Rolling over your old 401(k) is the best option if you can invest the money better in a personal IRA than you can in the old 401(k) or in your new

401(k). If you already work with an advisor, they will likely be able to manage that account for you as well. There are a lot of options here, but 401(k) providers typically have a very limited slate of investments and you can find a more complete, lower cost account elsewhere.

Whatever you do, don't just leave those drips and drabs of retirement plans hanging out unattended. Most people change jobs three times by the time they're 30 years old, so that could be three different 401(k)s. Make your life easier by consolidating plans. Do it as soon as you move to the next job so you don't forget and end up with a trail of accounts and investments that aren't working together to help you reach your goals.

Taking Money Out While You're Still Working for the Employer

It's difficult to take money out of your 401(k) if you're still working for the employer. The only way you can access it is if your employer allows loans. Not all plans do. Again, you have to go back to the contract—it's called a Summary Plan Description—to find out whether your plan will allow for any kind of loan (usually it's a hardship loan).

We strongly discourage anybody from doing this, because you're going to cost yourself the growth of the money. In addition, when you retire and want to access your money, you'll have to clear out any loan balances that are still hanging out... And, interest on those balances adds up, so it could be a shock to see what you owe after letting any loans ride for years on end. Instead, make this option a last resort. Instead, consider a home equity loan. Ask a friend. Ask a family member. Tap every other resource before you hit your 401(k).

It's only when you leave a job and roll your account to an IRA that you have the option to take money out. If you take it out before you're 59 and a half, there is a 10% penalty, and on top of that whatever you take out is going to be subject to income tax based on your income tax bracket. Therefore, if you take money out before you're 59 and a half, about a third of it will have to go back to Uncle Sam the next time you file your taxes.

There is one little loophole in the law that allows you to take money out before you're 59 and a half, and it's called the SEPP (Substantially Equal Periodic Payments). This allows you to tap into that money before you are 59 and a half, but it requires a mathematical calculation. You have to work with your CPA, and there's a limit on how much you can take out. For those facing early retirement or company buyouts, this may be one way to start getting the cash you need without facing penalties.

While most company plans have the 59 and a half rule, some plans use age 55 as the magic number—back to the Summary Plan Description. If your plan allows withdrawals before 59 and a half, you may be better off leaving that with your old employer and using the extra few years to withdraw penalty-free.

What Happens to Your 401(k) Account When You Retire?

It depends on your plan as to whether or not you have to take your money out when you quit your job. Some plans will say in the plan document, for instance, that any account with less than $5,000 will automatically be sent out to you. Some plans, though, will allow you to keep your account there. More employers now are trying to encourage employees to take their money and go. They don't want to have those extra administrative costs and responsibilities. That's where the rollover IRA comes in. Remember, set up an IRA account first, then do the paperwork to get your funds moved over without incurring a penalty.

Finding Accounts from Former Employers

We tend to have four or five jobs over the course of our careers, and more and more people are leaving these little bits and pieces of 401(k)s scattered around. You really need to take them with you. Either move the account to your new employer's plan or roll it to an IRA. Start to combine these so that you can keep an eye on them and ensure you are choosing the best investments. Often when you roll to an IRA, you have the ability to choose from a wider spread of funds instead of being limited to a plan's menu.

As of right now, there's not a central agency to call if you think you may have left a 401(k) behind from a former employer. We've heard of plans to have a searchable database available online in the future. We'll keep our fingers crossed that this pans out, but in the meantime, if you think you may have left a retirement account behind, go back through your work history and check with your old employers. Look through your records and see if you've received account statements. It's up to you to track down those lost pieces. This is one of the reasons it's important to move 401(k)s as soon as you change employers. Don't risk forgetting about your retirement accounts.

Annual Review

OK, you've got it. Can you forget it?

Hopefully! The idea with 401(k)s now is that you can set them and forget them. You can set your contribution to automatically raise up to your target savings rate, and you can set investments to rebalance to your original allocation periodically. All of these tools mean that without a major change in your situation, your account should be adequate without any more input from you.

However, we advise you to do a deep dive into your personal financial situation at least once a year, and the 401(k) is an important part of that plunge. If you have not had a major change in your life, won the lottery, lost all of your worldly belongings or planned a retirement party for yourself, you probably won't need to make any changes. But, here are a few things to look at in an annual review:

- Are you contributing enough? Are you hitting the 17% target? Can you contribute more?

- Have the investments changed in your plan? Plan menus do change, and if an old option is not available, search for the next best alternative. If your plan had target date options, it is unlikely that these have changed without keeping you up with the times.

- Do the investments work with your total portfolio? You cannot view your 401(k) in isolation. It is an asset like your other assets and needs to be viewed in that context. Say you have $100,000 in your 401(k) and $100,000 in outside investments and your overall allocation, based on your needs and risk tolerance, is 50% stocks 50% bonds. If both accounts are 50/50, fine, but if your outside investments are all stocks, then your 401(k) should be all bonds.

But Wait, I Don't Have a 401(k)!

As we said, retirement is the biggest financial decision that most people make. It's important that you prepare for it, and by "prepare," we mean save money. Self-employed workers or people not covered by a 401(k) or other retirement plan at work have other options.

A SIMPLE IRA and a SEP IRA are designed for small employers. 401(k)s can sometimes be expensive for the employer. There is a cost for the plan and for the administrators, and there are annual reporting requirements. Smaller employers usually cannot afford these expenses.

SIMPLE IRAs are for any employer with 100 or fewer employees. There's no formal plan. You have only an IRS form with a few simple boxes to check (no pun intended) that indicates how the account works. These plans have standard provisions and give small companies a way to help employees save for retirement without breaking the bank. In return, there are some limitations to the plan.

SIMPLE IRAs are salary-deferral plans, meaning you decide whether or not to contribute through your paycheck. Your employer commits to one of two possible matches—2% or 3%. Most opt for 3%. SIMPLE IRAs require immediate vesting, even on the match. This means no matter how long you stay with the company—one month, two years, etc.—ALL the money in the account is yours. In addition, the SIMPLE IRA has lower maximums that can be contributed than a 401(k). Right now, the annual maximum contribution is $12,500 for those under 50. These annual amounts change, so check the IRS website each year.

If you are a self-employed worker and only have to worry about yourself, the SEP IRA is probably the way to go. Contributions can vary widely from year to year, with the current maximum at a whopping $55,000 (2018) or 25% of your income. Most wait until the end of the year to see what they can afford to put aside, based on the last year's income and their current cash on hand. Know that if you have employees, the percentage that goes into YOUR account must also be the same percentage that goes into THEIR accounts. As with SIMPLE IRAs, there is immediate vesting with these accounts, so be careful with funding.

Many companies start as one woman (or one man) operations but later add employees as the company grows. You can change from a SEP IRA to a SIMPLE IRA or to a 401(k) to grow with your employees. Check with an advisor on the best option for you and on how to change retirement plans without raising red flags with the IRS.

If your company doesn't have a plan, open a personal IRA. This can be either a Traditional IRA (pre-tax) or a Roth IRA (post-tax). Traditional IRAs have pretty low income limits in order to get the tax deduction, but those only apply if your employer offers a retirement plan. For younger workers and people who will face a higher tax bracket in the future, the Roth IRA is the best deal available in tax avoidance. You pay taxes on your contributions now, while you are in a low tax bracket, but you will never pay taxes on that money again, even when the account has grown and you withdraw it in your wonderful golden retirement.

Keep in mind that you can layer plans. Have a 401(k) at work? Consider also setting up a Roth IRA. Have a small company on the side in addition to your work at a big corporation? Set up a SEP IRA for your side business while also funding the 401(k). You may bump into income contribution limits and total contribution limits with this, but you can save in taxes while saving for your retirement. Check with your CPA or financial advisor.

You can also convert a Traditional IRA to a Roth IRA. The big disadvantage to the conversion is that whatever you convert is counted as income: If you take $100,000 in a regular IRA and convert it to a Roth IRA this year, then that's going to be $100,000 of pure income that next year you have to pay tax on. That tax bill can be hard to swallow. You will also need to leave it in place for five years in order to start drawing on the account if you want to keep the tax-free advantage of the Roth. There are some qualifiers to this rule. Some people that we work with are doing what we call 'partial conversions.' Instead of, say, converting $100,000 in one year, they convert $10,000 a year for a few years. Having a nice little pot of tax-free money to dip your hands into at will is worth the little bit of tax bite in this strategy. Again, check with that CPA. You want to do it in such a way as to avoid hitting a higher tax bracket. One big advantage to the conversion is that the growth of the account and your future withdrawals become tax-free. A second big advantage is that you are not going to be obliged to take those required minimum distributions (RMDs) when you hit 70 and a half.

Don't Sabotage Your Savings

It can be tempting to take money out of your retirement savings. Say you leave one job and start a new one. Instead of rolling that 401(k) balance over, you decide to withdraw it and go on a trip. Sounds fun until you realize that now you have to start all over again building your retirement savings. Keep in mind that you don't get to take the money out without paying taxes on it. On top of that, you've erased the possibility that those funds can grow and wiped out the magic of compounding. So, hands off! If you want to take a trip or buy a new car, budget for it.

Don't make it harder than it already is. Give yourself a light at the end of the tunnel. Be your future self's own angel investor.

There you have it. Retirement is a big decision, and it's important that you are well-prepared to face it. There are a number of tools available, and the 401(k) is fast evolving to be one of the best. There are a lot of features and facets to consider, so be careful and work with a professional if you have any questions. Most importantly, however, save!

As a Wise P.I.G.G.Y. Once Said:

- When it comes to your retirement, you're on your own! Don't expect a pension or Social Security to bail you out.

- When you start your first job, sign up to contribute at least 10% of your paycheck.

- You need to contribute 16.9% every year for 30 years to replace working income so work your way up to this amount.

- Use your employer plan first. Then consider Traditional IRAs, Roth IRAs and taxable accounts to build savings.

- The employer match is NOT your maximum contribution.

- Learn about the mutual funds and exchange traded funds in the plan menu so you can make an informed choice.

- Review your accounts annually. Increase contributions and adjust the fund choices as needed.

- NEVER take a loan against your retirement plan.

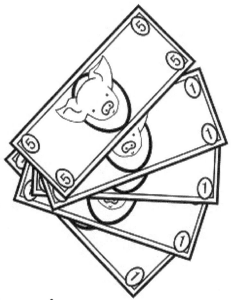

Get an education.

What is the Benefit of Higher Education?

A college education has worked its way into the American Dream fairly well ever since the end of WWII sent 7.8 Million veterans to college. This inflow of new students and tuition money greatly expanded the capacity of schools and broadened the pool of applicants. Now, about a third of current jobs require a bachelor's degree, and an estimated 65% of job openings will require some college education by the year 2020.

Not only are more jobs requiring higher educational attainment than ever before, those jobs are also offering higher pay than others. While there are certainly cases of highly skilled jobs with lower education requirements making high salaries, in general, there is still a positive correlation between educational attainment and income opportunity. According to US Census Bureau data, in 2010, a bachelor's degree meant an extra $20,000 in annual income compared to someone with only a high school diploma. A master's or professional degree helped even more—doubling or tripling the median full-time income. Getting a Ph.D. is a mixed bag and may not be the income booster that an MBA or law degree appears to provide.

Now when you hear people say that college is an investment in your future, you know what they mean. College is an investment that can result in a much higher income over your entire working life. That sounds great, right? Let's look at how you can make that investment in yourself or start planning for your kids' college costs.

529 Savings Plans

When we talk about the cost of college, financial advisors will often talk about the importance of saving. This is natural for us to do, because it involves some pretty easily calculable things. You know how much you want to save (or you can guess), and you know the timeline (roughly...as long as you know how old your child is, then you have an idea of when they will go to college). 529 plans make it easy for us to say something like: If you save $100/month in the target date plan option, then you will likely have around $35,000 when your child starts school. If you just want to pre-pay tuition, Mississippi offers a nice pre-paid plan called MPACT that lets you lock in tuition prices at current rates for a single transparent price based on the age of the child, the number of credit hours and what type of education you want to pay for. These are easy and natural things for a financial advisor to talk about.

Check out the 529 plan that your state offers. If you open this account for your children, it's a great way to have friends and relatives give monetary gifts to that child in a defined way. When it comes to student aid, money being in the 529 plan will not count against need-based aid as much as other assets or income may.

Student Loans

The other topic that comes up a lot, especially now, is student loans. Student loans are nearly unavoidable these days. We hear on the news about cases where people have student loan debt in the six figures and no great job prospects. There are a handful of payment choices to consider for repaying student loans and a few options to weigh, but these loans are a finite problem. You can deal with them. In general, income-based repayment plans are an excellent option. Be careful about taking out the loans, and be prompt with your payments.

If you need loans to pay for school, do not be afraid of them. If used well, this will be some of the best debt you take on in your life. For many people, a university education will have a high return on investment, and if you can borrow at fixed rates to fund that investment, all the better. Don't be afraid of the debt, just be very careful about the amount you use.

Student Loan Repayment

It's important to understand all of the terms of your student loans. Subsidized loans do not accrue interest while you are in school. Most loans do not require repayment until you have been out of school for six months. You can apply for deferments and extended grace periods as well. Keep in mind that interest may be accruing even if you are in a grace period.

Most student loans also offer unique repayment terms. The default repayment is typically a fixed, amortizing term. This means that each month you make the same monthly payment, which consists of interest and principal. The principal part of your payment will start small, but as you chip away at your balance, the interest part of the payment shrinks. With a fixed term, amortizing repayment plan, the only choice you have to make is how long you want to be making payments. It's most common to have a ten year repayment plan. If you are offered a longer plan with lower monthly payments, be aware that your total interest paid over the life of the loan will be higher.

Another payment plan is the graduated plan. Your payments will always be equal to or greater than your interest accrued and will increase every two years. This goes on for ten years when the loan is scheduled to be paid off.

The most unique repayment plans are income-based. There are several different names for the plans available, but they all take your income into account when calculating your monthly payment. These will always be the most affordable payments, and can potentially be less than your interest accrued. If your payment is less than your interest accrued, the interest will add to your balance and you may have to pay it later. Under many income-based repayment plans, your balance will be forgiven after a certain number of years of faithful payments. These can potentially be a boon for those who have a high debt burden and a low income.

Depending on your industry or employer, you may be eligible for student loan forgiveness. Check with your state and check the terms of your loan to see if there are any forgiveness programs available to you.

When you start down the path of repaying your student loans, make sure you are looking at ALL of your options. Look into what the monthly payment will be under each option and how long you will be paying on the loan. The Department of Education has a useful repayment calculator on their website. If your aim is to have the loans forgiven at some point in the future, make sure you are enrolled in the correct repayment plan. You don't want to find out years in the future that you're ineligible for forgiveness because you checked the wrong box. That is not a happy place to find yourself.

For what it's worth, we don't think student loans are the problem. It's the cost of college that's the problem. With that in mind, let's turn to the more interesting, more complicated third pillar of educational funding. This involves directly reducing the cost of college through finding the right college, getting a better offer and tinkering with your financial aid eligibility. We will generously call this "everything else."

Everything Else

With the average cost of college brushing up against $10,000 for an in-state public university, $24,000 for out of state or $33,000 for a private college, plus another $10,000 for room and board and a few thousand for other expenses, it's easy to see that this is a HUGE financial decision. Furthermore, it is a HUGE financial decision that is placed largely in the hands of a high school student who doesn't really understand all of the implications. Getting a discount on the sticker price can translate into big savings.

Set a Limit

Let's go ahead and get this out of the way: One way to reduce the cost of college is for the parent to just put his or her foot down. If you've looked at your budget, sized up your assets and have a solid grasp of what you can afford, just put an upper limit on what you're willing and able to spend and let that limit be the law. But beyond cutting off heads, let's look at what can be done to reduce the price you pay, both now and in the future!

There's a lot of talk about making sure you select a major that will land you a good paying job when you graduate. This is important, of course, and students should pay attention to this as they think about how the courses they choose to study in college will help to qualify them for their professions. But the classes and the major aren't the only items to consider. It's more than just the academics at the school—it's also the people and the network. If there's a specific company you want to work for, find out which schools that company has relationships with. Where do they recruit key personnel from? Some schools have reputations for sending graduates to work in specific industries. This is important and should not be ignored. Getting a return out of your college investment should be kept in mind as a key, if not a primary, goal.

Community College

A classic way of reducing the cost of college for most people is to attend a community college first. This will benefit most college bound high schoolers. Higher achieving students who have taken AP classes and Dual Enrollment classes may not have much left to get out of community college, but almost everyone else may see a clear benefit. Not only is community college tuition less expensive, but there are also initiatives underway to make it free! And scholarships based on ACT scores are pretty straightforward with most Mississippi community colleges. Savings can also come from living at home. It's a practical possibility since most community colleges have multiple convenient locations.

Community college may not be for everyone. As we mentioned, if you've already taken a lot of college courses or have credit through AP exams, you may see less benefit than others who have followed the standard high school requirements. Community college is an excellent choice for those not ready for full time university. Likewise, for students planning to continue on to a state university, completing general course requirements at a community college can be a great decision before heading to state.

Choose a School that Wants YOU

One huge way to reduce the price tag on college is to focus on the school itself. This doesn't mean simply looking at which school has the lowest sticker price or has the best financial aid packages in general. Look for which school will give YOU the best offer. While many people grow up wanting to go to a specific school or may think a specific school has the program that is just right for them, there are about 2,500 public and private four year institutions in America, and a few of them are looking for exactly what you have going for you. Instead of looking for what school you want, see if there are any schools out there that want YOU. Working with a professional admissions counselor can help identify those schools looking for your combination of academic successes and extracurricular skills. If you are an ideal candidate for a school, they will make you a better offer than you see advertised. Keep an open mind when applying to schools you may not have thought about attending before. You could be in for a treat!

If you can't find or afford a professional admissions counselor, there are some resources that can help you figure out who wants you the most. College Navigator is a resource managed by the National Center for Educational Statistics that can help you sort through schools. College Data (dot com) has a range of resources that can show you which colleges you are an ideal fit for and provides useful guides for the daunting application process.

Work Study vs. Co-Op

Work study programs are great, but you will have to assess for yourself if it makes sense for you to work full-time while in school. A better option may be co-op years or semesters. Co-op is particularly common in science and engineering courses. Essentially, the student takes a year or semester off to work in the industry. This gives you a paycheck, work experience and college credit as well as the possibility of tuition reimbursements or even a job offer! If you are considering a future in engineering or hard sciences, look for schools that have strong industry connections and advertise co-op options.

Scholarships, Leases and Transcripts

Leaning more towards the financial side of things, students should definitely apply for scholarships! Local and regional scholarships are harder to find, but are typically much less competitive. Apply to local civic organizations, such as the Rotary Club, to find community organizations willing to support your college education. While they can be difficult to find, many websites aggregate scholarships from all over the country to help you cut through the mess.

If you are applying to a program that is not offered in your state, the Southern Regional Education Board has a Common Market throughout 15 Southeastern states that gives you in-state tuition if your state does not offer the program you want. Since out-of-state tuition can tack on $10,000 or more to your education bill, this can be a huge savings.

If your student is in private housing (renting an apartment while they are in school), the lease probably runs for the full calendar year, not just the academic year. This means you are paying rent over the summer too! Turn this into money spent wisely. Instead of moving home and taking it easy all summer, encourage your student to get a job in town or take summer courses at the university or a nearby community college. Summer school is a good way to knock out some classes to make sure graduation is on time. So, if you're paying for a full year apartment lease, you may as well get some value out of it!

Keep in mind that EVERYTHING students do in high school matters. The high school transcript is a clean slate for incoming freshmen, so get them focused on the bigger goal of finding and funding a college education by 9th grade at the latest! Older siblings or family friends in college may be an excellent resource for your high schooler to use as an example to begin to truly understand the importance of their academic achievements.

This may also be a useful tactic in the debt conversation. You can sit down with your teenager and explain what debt is and how they might end up with $100,000 worth of debt or more. Of course, it may still seem a little abstract to them. So, again, if you have a family friend or older sibling who can explain to them what it means to carry that debt, your teen may get the picture more clearly and have a little more respect for the total cost of college—regardless of who is paying for it. This goes back to just putting your foot down on the total cost as well. If you explain to your child that you simply cannot afford the school they want to go to, work with them to find a lower cost option.

Going to college is one of the biggest financial decisions that you can make, and much of it is in the hands of a high school student that, however smart, probably doesn't truly appreciate the ramifications of the decision. Most financial advisors will focus on the savings aspect of college, because that part of college planning is familiar. We also focus on existing debt burdens since they're unavoidable. The middle area of reducing the sticker price is complex and tends to happen very quickly. A lot of research and preparation must go into it to make sure you're getting the best deal. But with the cost of four years of university education ranging from $80,000 to $200,000, getting a discount on the front end can be immensely valuable.

Organizing Your Finances

Since we're on the topic, here are some ways that you can play around on the edges with your income and assets to make sure that you get the student aid that you need. These are the basic, sensible ways to organize your finances in the years before sending a child to college.

- Understand the FAFSA! The FAFSA is where asset and income information of parents and students is compiled. Different assets and sources of income are weighted to produce an "expected family contribution." This number is subtracted from the cost of college to find out how much financial aid your student may need. Structuring your income and assets in a way that decreases your expected family contribution will raise the amount of financial aid that your student is eligible for.

- The best owner for a 529 savings plan is the parent. This is important for legal reasons of ownership so that the parent retains control in the event the situation changes. This is also important for the FAFSA. If the account is in the parent's name, it is an asset of the parents, counting the least towards the family contribution and the withdrawals do not count as income. If it were an asset of grandparents or someone other than the parent or the student, withdrawals would count as income of the student, drastically reducing the amount of financial aid they'd be eligible for.

- The FAFSA form takes an earlier year's tax information now. The earlier availability is nice (October), but it means you have to start shifting income and assets around even earlier. If you are planning on maxing out IRAs and 401(k)s to reduce your FAFSA exposure, do it a few years in advance.

- If your child has investment savings of their own, spend those down a few years before the FAFSA comes up. Money in UGMA/UTMA accounts must be spent on the child, but it's a pretty flexible area of spending. You want to get your child's assets down to a minimal level as they count about 20% against financial aid.

- Having grandparents or other family members chip in for school costs is nice but can come at a steep price. As in the above example of a 529 plan being owned by a grandparent, you want to make sure that the gift does not count as income of the student. If it will count, you may want them to delay making the gift until the last two years of college. This way, it won't affect the FAFSA while the student is still in school. Alternatively, you could hold the money until after college and use it to pay down loans quickly.

As a Wise P.I.G.G.Y. Once Said:

- On average, college graduates have higher lifetime earnings and lower unemployment rates.

- Salary and availability of job opportunities vary depending on the degree you earn and the reputation of the college from which you graduate. Do your research.

- Organize your finances in a way that best prepares you or your child for financial aid.

- Don't be afraid of taking out student loans, but do exercise caution on the amount you take out. Remember that just because you are allowed to take out a certain amount, this doesn't mean you are required to use it all.

- Keep in mind that student loans are often not forgiven in a bankruptcy. The debt stays with you.

- If at all possible, sign up for automatic payments from your bank account to repay your student loans. This can save you 0.25% in interest and ensure that you don't miss a payment.

- Make sure that you are in the best repayment plan for your situation.

- Look for ways to limit the cost of college. Consider taking basic courses at a community college. Go after scholarships. Find a school that wants YOU as a student.

- If you're planning for your child's future, 529 Savings Plans are generally an excellent tool to use. And, if you need help navigating college expenses, consult an expert.

Decide where to live.

We all need a place to live. The question is: Should we buy a house or just rent a place? That depends.

When you rent, you're spending money you don't expect to get back. Once you write the rent check, that money is gone never to reappear.

Renting is often your only option when you're young and just starting out. It's also a good option if you want to be flexible. Buying a house commits you to a location for a fairly long period of time. You can't just notify the landlord when you want to move. Instead, you have to find someone willing to buy your house. How easy that is depends on your location, the price you're asking for your house and the overall market. You may recall 2008 and the housing crisis. If you owned your home, then you were probably unable to sell your home.

Even in good markets, homeownership comes with buying and selling costs. Overcoming those to end up with a few dollars in your pocket typically requires about 3 to 5 years. Moving more often than that will eat into the equity you've built into that home.

If you anticipate moving in a short period of time or if you're just not certain about THIS one place, rent. Even if you want to stay in one locale, you may not know the best neighborhoods until you've hung around for a while. So, rent and research.

Once you decide to put down roots and have saved enough for a down payment, then consider buying a house. For most of us, a home is one of our biggest investments, and outside of that awful housing crisis and meltdown in 2008, houses have been good investments. While we all know that one person who turned a 50% profit in short order, that's not the norm in real estate. Expect 3 to 5% per year, on average.

While that doesn't sound like a lot, the beauty of homeownership is that it acts like a piggy bank. Most of us will take out a mortgage to afford a home. This means we don't own the WHOLE house until the final payment is made. But unlike rent, every time you make a house payment, you're building up equity, or ownership, in the house. You're paying down the loan and owning a bit more of your home with each passing month. This is why the 3 to 5 year rule of thumb is a good one. It takes this long to really start to make headway on your mortgage and to build up a greater share of the ownership. And it's forced savings. If you don't make the house payment, you lose your place to live. Keep making it and you might end up owning the front door and the back patio.

How Do You Get Ready for Homeownership?

You're considering buying a home. It's what your parents did. It's what your friends have done. Isn't this what everybody does?

There are two things you need to do. First, you need to get your credit in tip-top shape. Request an up-to-date report to pinpoint any problems. If you're now married or in a relationship and considering buying a house with your partner, swap reports. If both names will be on the house, both of you will need excellent credit scores to proceed.

Depending on your credit problems, expect to spend about a year preparing for the big purchase. This gives you time to beef up that score. Of course, if you have some big items (like bankruptcy) or even small items (like missed payments), it could take much longer to get your score squared away.

Consider going through a pre-approval process. This doesn't guarantee you'll qualify for the mortgage, but this gives you an idea of what is possible. Based on preliminary information, the lender may estimate the maximum mortgage allowed.

How Much House Can You Afford?

The question we always hear is: How much house can I afford? You don't want to be "house poor," because you want to be able to do other things with your money besides pay for the roof over your head. But there are some rules of thumb. We often say that the total purchase price can be two and a half times your household income or that you can use 31% of your gross income for that mortgage payment every month. Or, you can include all of your debt and make that mortgage payment 43% of your gross income. We usually try to go below that amount—again, to give you some wiggle room.

If you work with a realtor, know that they will encourage you to hit the higher end of that range. After all, their commission is based on the home price—the more expensive the house, the more they make. In fact, they often will take you to the high-end place first, get you to say "Ahh, how beautiful!" and then take you to the realistic place where you feel letdown. Stick to your guns on what you can reasonably afford.

What about your down payment? That's where most people get hung up. Conventional loans require 20% down. So, if you're purchasing a $150,000 house, then that's $30,000 you have to come up with. That can be lot for a family to save up. Know that you can put down less than that, but anything less than 20% means that you're going to have to pay for mortgage insurance; and that's going to add about 1% annually. On a

$250,000 house, that means you're going to pay about $200 extra every month just to cover the mortgage insurance.

Some options on lower down payments:

- A Fannie Mae loan only requires 5%, but remember that you still have to pay for the mortgage insurance.

- FHA (Federal Housing Administration) loans require 3 ½%.

- Under FHA there's something called the Conventional 97 which only requires 3%.

- Then there is the Rural Housing Loan, also under the FHA. There's no down payment required for this. It is for low income buyers, and even though it says "rural," it's not just for rural areas.

- For those who serve in our military, we have a great program offering VA loans. There is no down payment and no mortgage insurance. Again, this program is only for those who serve in the military. The interest rate on the mortgage is usually 37 ½% below the market, too.

If you go ahead with a home purchase that includes the mortgage insurance, know that you can eventually petition to have that insurance dropped. The lender needs to make sure you have 20% skin in the game at all times. That means if you stay in the house long enough and the price appreciates high enough, you will eventually have a 20% share of the house, even if you only put down 10%.

How do you get the mortgage insurance dropped? Watch sales in the area around you for an idea of the market value of your house and then look at the principal owed on your house to estimate whether or not you've contributed 20%. You will need a new appraisal to prove your case, and you will have to pay for this appraisal. It will be worth it, though, if it saves you hundreds of dollars each year.

What about Other Costs?

After you've saved for the down payment and qualified for the mortgage, you may be patting yourself on the back. Not so fast! That's not all there is to it. Your monthly payment will be comprised of interest and principal that goes towards the payoff of the mortgage, but there are other costs to consider.

An escrow account will be set up by your lender, and they will collect extra money from you to cover property taxes and insurance. This protects their ownership in your house. Before you sign that purchase offer, make sure you understand what these additional costs will be and prepare ahead of time to pay for them.

If you live in the Northeast, property taxes can amount to thousands per month. Here in Mississippi, it's thousands per YEAR, amounting to $200 to $300 more per month on your payment. You can ask the realtor about these costs. They may appear on the seller's disclosure statement. If all else fails, call the county clerk and ask for a tax history on the house.

Know that some states discount property taxes for full-time residents. Some states discount taxes for senior citizens. But, some don't discount anything! Know the rules of the state in which you're buying.

Next, there's the home insurance. Call a local insurance agent and get a quote on the property. If the annual premium is $2,400, your lender will escrow another $200 per month to cover the bill. Add the mortgage payment to the property tax and to the insurance, and you'll see what your monthly payment will be. Unless you have an adjustable rate mortgage, expect the payment to the mortgage company to stay the same for the life of the loan. The other elements may change, though, and any changes in the annual billed amounts on taxes and insurance can drastically affect your monthly payment. Be prepared.

Regarding your insurance policy, make sure you read the contract and understand what it covers. Most of us don't want to pay more than we have to for coverage, but we do want to know we're covered if the worst happens. After all, this is a home we're talking about. Pay careful attention to the fine print and don't be afraid to ask questions about the policy. Run through a list of what-if situations and worst case scenarios, and then find out if you have the coverage you need if any of those events do happen.

Finally, know that there are additional costs to homeownership. If the air conditioning breaks, you can't call the landlord. When the weeds grow, you have to mow. When the toilet leaks, it's yours to repair. All the maintenance that had previously been the responsibility of your landlord is now on your shoulders. Keep in mind that older houses require more maintenance than brand new ones. Plan for additional expenses like furniture, appliances and HOA (Homeowner Association) fees.

How do you make sure you can handle whatever expenses pop up? Don't buy the MOST house you can afford, and always expect the unexpected. Remember that emergency fund? You will need it.

Fixed Rate vs. Adjustable Rate

Mortgages are offered in fixed or adjustable rates. The right one for you depends on the current market rate and on your own set of circumstances. Fixed rate mortgages don't change. Once the rate and payment are set, they stay the same for the entire life of the loan. Adjustable rate mortgages adjust according to some schedule. Read the fine print in your loan contract. A common adjustment is a five year step-up, with rates starting at one rate and then gradually moving to a higher rate over five years. Another type adjusts based on market rates, with a new rate calculated each year. There may be limitations on how much the rate can increase in a year. These mortgages are all over the place, so make sure you understand what you're getting into before you sign on the dotted line.

When rates are quite low (as they are now), fixed rate mortgages are the way to go. Why would you opt for an adjustable mortgage when you can lock in a low rate for 30 years? Most adjustable rate mortgages are lower than fixed rate ones, which is why some people are enticed by these even in low interest rate environments. Don't do it.

Adjustable rate mortgages are good options when rates are high, and you expect them to go down. They give you a break on the front-end with the hope of lower rates later. And, adjustable rate mortgages are good options for homeowners who don't think they'll be in the house for a long time. They expect to move before the rate rises to an unreasonable amount. So, for them, it's all about flexibility.

15 Years vs. 30 Years

Usually, you have two maturity options to choose from on your mortgage. You can go for a 30-year mortgage or a 15-year mortgage. Most people opt for a 30-year mortgage because of the affordability. Suppose you have a $150,000 mortgage. The rate is 5%. The 30-year loan means your combined principal and interest payment will be around $805. The 15-year loan means a payment of $1,186, or $381 more per month. That's a big difference!

If you're just starting out, you'll likely want to choose the 30-year mortgage. You'll be able to afford a decent house and have a reasonable monthly payment. You'll have a little room each month to afford the extras of homeownership. But as you age and build assets, consider moving to a 15-year loan. The cost savings over the long term are huge!

For that $150,000 mortgage, 30 years of payments of $805 means you'll end up paying a total of $289,800. Fifteen years of $1,186 cuts that bill to $213,480. Quite the savings! But, hey, we all have to do what we have to do. Opt for a monthly payment that won't choke you.

Is there a middle ground? Yes! Choose the 30-year loan, but make extra payments. If you make one extra payment a year on your mortgage, you'll cut off around 7 years of a 30-year loan. Of course, all this depends on the size of the loan and the interest rate. You can also simply apply a little extra to each payment or make lump sum additions to the loan. Got a bonus? Use half to pay down your mortgage. One caution—when making extra payments on your mortgage, keep good records. Make sure your lender applies these payments appropriately.

Should You Use a Realtor?

You should probably hire a realtor, especially if this is your first time purchasing a home. Typical realtor commissions are 6%. Yes, that can be negotiated, but expect to pay this much. The listing agent gets half, and the selling agent gets the other half. While it's important for you to be firm in the home price you can afford, the realtor can offer guidance on many things. Your realtor should be giving you inside information about the particular area where you're shopping. Look for a realtor who specializes in the neighborhoods you're interested in living. Also, look for a realtor with a proven track record.

The realtor will assist with the negotiations and will explain all costs to you. Closing costs are standard in most contracts, but there can be surprises. The agent will explain what is expected of you and will assist in all documentation. This person can't know everything about the house, but they want to make a repeat customer of you. And they want you to recommend them to your friends!

As you become more experienced, you may decide to go it alone. Be careful. Even the most seasoned homebuyer can get tripped up.

When Should You Refinance?

Congratulations! You've moved into your home, and you've started making those monthly payments. You're done, right? Wrong. You should always monitor interest rates. A site like Bankrate.com is a good resource to help you gauge the direction of rates. You'll be able to see average mortgage rates across the country for 15 and 30 year loans.

If rates drop significantly below your current rate, consider refinancing your mortgage. This means you will pay off your existing mortgage and get a new lower rate mortgage in its place. Some will say you should wait until the rate has dropped 2%. We say you need to calculate the payment.

There are costs involved in refinancing, so you need to make sure you can recoup those costs. How much longer do you plan to stay in the house? If you're moving next year, it might not be worth it, but if you plan to stick around for several years, then even a $100 savings per month can make it a reasonable choice. Start by calling your existing mortgage company and saying: I'm going to refinance. I want to give you the first shot at keeping my business. What can you do for me? Make sure they outline all costs. Then shop around. It's a competitive business.

Refinancing means going through the hassle of digging out information on all your accounts, going through an appraisal and signing all those forms (even if only digitally). But look at the savings! So forge ahead with that home purchase, but always keep your eye on interest rates.

Reverse Mortgage

A reverse mortgage is still a mortgage. It's a loan that is backed by the value of your house. Instead of you making payments every month to the lender, the lender pays YOU. Sounds like a great deal, huh? Not so fast!

Who can get a reverse mortgage? You must be 62 or older, and they are designed for people who already own their homes but need extra money. They need money right now. But, remember: they are loans! You'll be able to get about 60 - 75% of the value of the home. This can come as a lump sum, as monthly payments or as a line of credit. They can be very appealing, because you get to stay in your house; but you don't have to sell the house to unlock its value. There are no monthly payments like there are with most loans. However, the loan comes due at death or at the sale of the home.

There are some drawbacks associated with reverse mortgages. There are very high upfront fees, usually around 5%. They have high fixed rates—higher than with regular mortgages—and these rates are built into the value of the loan they are giving you. It drains the value of that home. It is a LAST resort to use only if you don't have other means to support you in the meantime. If you didn't save and invest while you were young, this could be the only way to get extra cash just to help you LIVE. So save and invest and avoid these if at all possible. As with all contracts, read the fine print.

Is there anything else you could do? If you need some money right now, you can consider a straight refinance of your home with a cash-out of the equity. Alternatively, you can do a straight line of credit.

Be very, very careful with reverse mortgages. Don't get tempted by celebrities advertising them online or on the television. Those stars have plenty of money, so they won't be using reverse mortgages themselves. You, on the other hand, can end up buying yourself a boatload of trouble. These are a last resort.

As a Wise P.I.G.G.Y. Once Said:

- Save up for a down payment and the upfront costs of purchasing a home. And keep an eye on your credit! This is not a time to make foolish mistakes.

- When purchasing home insurance, ask questions about the policy. Know what's covered and what's not.

- As a home owner, you are responsible for the costs to repair and maintain your home and yard. Budget for these expenses and build your emergency fund.

- Fixed rate mortgages are often the best choice, especially in low interest rate environments. Be very careful before choosing an adjustable rate.

- Select a loan term that works for your budget. Remember not to buy the MOST house possible.

- Use a realtor. Their expertise will guide you through the home-buying process and prevent you from making errors.

- Keep your eye on interest rates. You may find an opportunity to refinance your mortgage.

- A reverse mortgage is a last resort. As always, read the fine print.

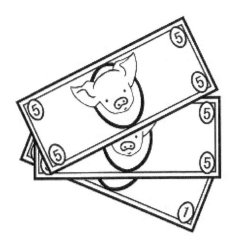

Choose your wheels wisely.

The first car Ryder owned was a 1999 Cadillac de Ville, white with blue leather interior. It could fit four adults comfortably on the front seat, and the trunk was spacious enough for him to move into his first house in two trips. Unfortunately, it was of an era less austere than the present, and that showed in its thirst for gasoline and oil. Frequent, expensive oil changes would often turn up costly repairs related to the oil. The car's history (it was once the unstoppable force that collided with a somewhat movable brick wall) also made it a looming liability. He swung the opposite way when he bought a Prius in the summer of 2016.

A Quick Note on Leasing vs. Buying

When you lease a car, you do not own it. This often gives you a lower monthly payment than if you take a loan out to buy the vehicle, but be very careful evaluating the deal. Traditionally, leases lower your monthly cost but raise your overall cost. That being said, sometimes manufacturers craft lease deals very attractively to entice more people to pick up their cars. Look at the total amount of payments and the purchase price at the end of the lease before jumping on one of these.

Buying a Vehicle

Unless you've saved up for a cheap used car, you're probably going to finance your purchase. As always when taking on debt, don't let the availability of cheap money tempt you into buying a more expensive car than you can really afford. Cars.com has a useful Affordability Calculator that can help you understand which vehicles work for your budget. Plug in a reasonable monthly payment that won't strain your pocketbook, and the calculator will tell you the maximum total cost for the vehicle that you should be willing to pay. The two main unknowns will be the term and the interest rate. The term is the length of time you will be paying the loan, and the interest rate is the cost of the loan. For calculation purposes, check a fairly short term like 36 months.

I prefer buying to leasing, but there's something in our human nature that makes us focus on how much we have to put down on the front-end versus total cost overall. We even think in terms of how much it costs us each month rather than the total cost, and this is why dealers can get us to agree to a lease. Usually, leasing costs less per month than buying, and the down payment for a lease is much smaller than for a purchase. You don't have a loan, so, at the end of the lease, you don't own the vehicle.

One of the disadvantages to a lease is that it does end. Every two to three years, you have to turn the car in and decide whether or not to get a new lease. This means there is no residual value. You have nothing when the lease is up. You can't trade it in. You just turn it in. There's nothing left. All kinds of penalties can be incurred with a lease. The biggest one of which is if you go over the set mileage. Typically, ten to fifteen thousand miles per year is all that you're allowed. If you use your car for work, you can easily drive more miles than that in a few years. Plus, if you return the car early, you're likely to be penalized. And, of course, if there are damages to the car, you're going to be penalized for that.

Do the math, and you'll likely find that in the long run, you're really better off buying your car outright—especially with current low interest rates and with the deals offered on cars right now. Vehicles are becoming even more reliable, too. They're lasting longer. Four or five years down the road when you no longer have the monthly loan payment, your car will most likely still have a lot of life left in it.

What Term Should You Agree To?

Having a longer term reduces your monthly payment, but can sometimes raise both your interest rate and the total amount you end up paying. You will likely be offered a range of term options. Common terms are 36, 48 and 60 month, though longer and shorter terms may be available. There is no hard and fast rule on how long of a term you should have, but the 36-60 month terms hit the sweet spot. If you get a term shorter than 36 months, it may make more sense just to save up for the car instead of borrowing for it. Anything longer than 60 months is risky because of the unknown of just what could possibly happen over that amount of time. In five years, you could change your mind about the car, get into an accident or simply need a new car. Having to pay a loan on a car you don't want to own is not a good feeling. Additionally, you are generally required to carry comprehensive insurance the entire time you have a loan on the car. Comprehensive insurance can be expensive. If you wanted to lower your car insurance costs (especially on a car several years old) you wouldn't be able to if you still held the loan.

What if the Interest Rate is Too High?

Auto loans are somewhat uniform, but there is room to play. The lowest rates you will be offered are often at your bank or at a large dealership. Check with your bank to see what rates they offer. This is a good practice anyway, because it lets you know what to expect. If you're not offered something comparable when you're outside of the bank, then you know to go back to the bank because you have better options there. If you can't get a good interest rate anywhere, you may need to revisit the affordability of the car altogether. Extending the term on a high interest loan just to lower your monthly payment drastically increases the amount of interest you pay.

With new car purchases, zero interest loans may be offered to get cars off the lot. These are often juxtaposed against cash back discounts. How do you decide which one is worth it? Look at the total payments you will make under each plan. Part of this may be determined by the monthly amount you can pay. The total amount paid, including interest and taking into account any discounts or fees, should give you the best comparison between offers.

What Other Costs Are There With a New Car?

When you buy a new car, you will also have to pay a host of fees and taxes. Depending on your state and local area tax structure, this could end up amounting to quite a lot and add to the total cost. Before you commit to a car, ask the dealer what sort of taxes and fees will be tacked on. There is no reason they can't give you a good estimate to factor in while you're shopping. Subtract fees and taxes from your maximum vehicle cost before continuing.

Keep in mind that some of these fees and taxes must be paid annually. You will also have to purchase insurance. If you're financing the car, you'll need comprehensive insurance. Check with your agent or an online outlet (most compare prices across insurers) to get an idea of how much your monthly payment will cost you. Again, remember to factor this expense in when calculating the affordability of the vehicle.

How Do You Reduce These Costs?

The biggest cost will be the price you pay for the car. Remember that the sticker price is the dealer's starting maximum, so don't rest until you've gotten yourself a discount. We won't tell you how to negotiate—there are plenty of resources online to teach you how to do that—but be sure to do it. We've heard of people sending written requests for a specific vehicle to dozens of dealerships just to see which one offered the best deal. When Ryder bought his Prius, he just happened upon someone who needed to hit a quota at the end of the quarter and negotiated against himself as Ryder silently test drove the car. Whatever negotiating tactics you decide to try out, put in the effort to reduce the price you pay.

To get a deal on his Prius, Ryder researched his options and made a spreadsheet to calculate the value of each. He knew what he wanted when he walked into the dealership. He had already gotten a quote for his new insurance rates and was prepared to cover the cost, and he used the same insurance company he'd had for a while because the transition was seamless. He had a good idea of the rates available from his bank and from other lenders and was pleasantly surprised when his rate came in a tiny bit below the expected rate.

New vs. Used

The biggest price difference is between new and used cars. You probably know that used cars can be much, much cheaper than new cars. The amount of depreciation, or value lost, by a new car varies between makes and models, but it can be a significant amount of the price of the car. Ryder was able to get a $25,000 car for less than $17,000 even though it was only six months old. That's savings he couldn't have gotten simply through negotiation. When buying any car, you're buying the future miles you're going to drive it. For the same price, a car that's expected to drive more miles will be worth more to you than a car that won't make it as far. This makes new cars more valuable, but there is also a "new car premium" that can't be explained in cold dollar terms. If you don't have a hugely emotional connection to your car, you can save a lot of money by buying used.

When looking at used cars, you'll need to do more research. Check Consumer Reports reviews to see if any particular year was more problematic than the rest. For a car that has been produced for a while, redesign years in which they made a lot of changes often have the lowest reliability ratings. Avoiding those particular years can help you avoid potential problems lurking under the hood.

Get a report on the car to find out if it has been involved in any accidents. You want to know the type of repair work that has been done on the vehicle and whether or not the car has been regularly serviced. Consider taking it to a trusted mechanic for a check-up before committing to the purchase.

Insurance

You will be required to carry a minimum liability coverage on your new car. This is the most basic level of insurance. Liability insurance covers damage that you cause to other people, their property or their vehicles in an accident. If you're worried about being hit by an uninsured motorist, you can get fairly cheap uninsured motorist insurance that will cover damage to your property or person in the event of an accident.

Beyond the basics, there's collision and comprehensive insurance. Collision insurance covers damage to your own vehicle even if you cause the accident or if the other motorist doesn't have adequate coverage. Collision insurance covers your car, so the value of it is limited to the value of your car. Comprehensive insurance covers other damage to your car and may include theft, vandalism and damage in a disaster. If you have a loan on your car, you may be required to keep comprehensive and collision insurance on the car.

Your insurance may come with some hidden benefits. It's fairly common for insurance to cover some sort of roadside assistance. Many comprehensive policies will give you a free windshield repair each year. Ryder's policy also covers replacement of keys and any harm to pets in an accident. These extra benefits may be repeated elsewhere too, so check your policy to make sure you're not paying someone else for duplicate coverage.

Buying a car can surprise you with hidden costs and options. Do plenty of research beforehand so that you know what to expect and can negotiate properly. Make sure you get the necessary insurance, but don't pay for coverage you don't need. Once you've bought your car, take care of routine maintenance to avoid costly repairs.

RVs

RVs tempt many people, but before you head out to the lot to start shopping, stop and ask yourself a few questions. The first is: Can you afford it? If you're thinking about paying for it with cash, remember that by giving up that cash, especially if you're retired, you're giving up some protection for yourself. If you want to finance the purchase, consider the overall cost of debt.

Another question to ask yourself is: Should you? Will you actually use it? Rather than purchasing an RV outright, try out the experience first by renting one and taking it on a trip.

Keep in mind that an RV is usually not cheaper than a hotel. When you add in fuel, lot rental, maintenance and repairs, you'll discover that you're paying about the same amount—sometimes more.

Look at the initial cost, too. There's a high mark-up on new RVs. That means you really need to negotiate. As soon as you drive that RV off the lot, it's going to depreciate by about a third. That means you need to consider a used RV. Low mileage is common because, again, a lot of people buy an RV thinking they're going to use it, and they never do. Know that there are plenty out there with low mileage.

Consider the maintenance costs. Do you have room on-site where you're living to store your RV? Many people have to pay for extra storage. Then, there's insurance costs, and RVs must be maintained and will need repairs.

When it comes to financing, RVs are treated like second homes. This means you get a tax deduction on the interest. However, that only applies to the RV or the camper. If you have a camper and you have a truck to tow it, you don't get the tax break on the truck.

These are luxury items, but the interest rates and the time on the loan will be very similar to what you'd expect to get on a car. That means the terms of the loan are heavily dependent on your credit score. The better your score, the better the rate on the loan. Bear in mind that when you finance an RV, because of depreciation, it's very common to end up owing more than the value of that RV. Be careful.

Some alternatives to purchasing an RV outright: Consider renting. Renting is a good way to just try it out before you buy. Some people opt for shared ownership. With this, the RV is used more often, and the cost is not as burdensome.

As a Wise P.I.G.G.Y. Once Said:

- Choose carefully before leasing a vehicle.

- Don't buy more car than you can afford.

- Budget insurance into your monthly payment.

- Compare interest rates from lenders.

- Remember that the biggest price savings is opting for used over new.

- Save for repairs and tires. Service your vehicle regularly.

Get covered.

Insurance

The whole point of insurance is to cover the big "what ifs" in life. What if you wreck your car? What if you get sick? What if you can't work? What if you die and your family loses your income? Hopefully, you're covered on the little "what ifs." What if the AC goes out? What if the car needs new tires? Those you can cover yourself, especially if you've been saving in your emergency fund. That's all to say that you don't need insurance for EVERY thing that could happen, and you may not need insurance forever and always. Things change.

But you need to consider all the big events that could wreck your finances, and you need to regularly consider how you can protect against these opportunities for misfortune.

There are three types of losses covered by insurance: loss of income, loss of property and loss of health.

Loss of Income: Disability Insurance

Disability insurance is something most people don't think about. They wonder: What happens if I die? Their solution to cover the possibility of their deaths: I need life insurance to protect my family. More people, more often than not, are going to face disability. One in four will have a chance of becoming disabled, and the average duration of that disability is three years. That's a lot of time to lose income!

Here's an interesting stat: About 40% of mortgage defaults are due to a disability. So, the question becomes: How do you replace lost income?

Social Security does have a disability program. It's through SSDI or SSI. You can apply online at www.socialsecurity.gov or call their 800 number (1-800-772-1213). It's not easy to qualify, and the process takes quite a while.

If you have a terminal illness, you automatically qualify for disability through Social Security. If it's not terminal, though, it has to be a disability that lasts longer than one year. You will have to go through an application process requiring medical records. This can take anywhere from three to five months, and we're hearing of long delays on getting qualified for this program. Your payment is based on your earnings record. If you have dependents, they may qualify for payments. Your disability is going to be reassessed every five years. The good news on this is if you are on Social Security Disability after two years, you automatically qualify for Medicare, so your health insurance is covered at that time.

Know that this program is only for people who are currently in the workforce. We often get the question: Can you apply for disability if you are retired? The answer is no.

The bigger issue with disability is that you need money NOW, and SSI may not be enough or you may not qualify for it. That's where disability insurance can come in. Many of us can get disability insurance through our employers who often offer this type of insurance. It will replace 50-60%

of your income, but there may be an offset if you apply for Social Security. It may be more important (well, we think it is more important) than life insurance. You really need to look at your situation and ask yourself what will happen if you cannot work. Who will replace that income? How will it be replaced?

Look at the Disability Insurance Resource Center (www.di-resource-center.com) to research information. This will give you all kinds of statistics and guidelines on disability. Start thinking about whether or not you need disability insurance in addition to depending on Social Security. While life insurance for single people is often not needed, this isn't the case with disability insurance. If you're working and you'll be in a bind if you can't work and earn money, you need disability insurance.

Shop around. Read the fine print. Know that if the time comes when you have to use that policy, you'll probably run into some walls. After all, the insurance company profits more by paying you less. Choose a good company and a good policy.

Loss of Income: Life Insurance

Don't buy life insurance for children. Life insurance is to protect against loss of income. How many four year olds are hoofing it to work every day? Some will say: Oh, but it will cover a funeral. First, the odds of that four year old dying are slim (thank goodness), and second, there are better ways to cover funeral costs. Beef up your emergency fund, or put the money in a savings account.

The purpose of life insurance is to protect those left behind when the family loses an earner. This means each adult should be protected. Even the stay-at-home parent should have some protection. After all, if that person dies, a paid person will have to step in to take over those duties. That stay-at-home person represents an earnings offset.

How much life insurance is enough? That depends on your family's needs and current lifestyle. One rule of thumb is to purchase insurance with a payoff of ten times your current income. If you're making $50,000 per year, a $500,000 policy should be enough.

Some will recommend adding another $100,000 for each child still at home. That offers an additional pad to cover the education of younger children.

Another approach is called DIME. DIME stands for Debt, Income, Mortgage and Education. Determine how much debt (besides your house) you have. Consider how many years your family will need to replace your current income. How much is left on your mortgage? And how much will be needed to cover those children until college graduation? It's a more complete picture.

Once you decide on the appropriate amount for you and your family, you must delve into the sleep-inducing world of insurance. Aim for using term policies. These cover only a certain time period—10, 15, 20 years—when your family is more vulnerable. They are cheaper than other forms of insurance and are usually the best way to go. Avoid whole life and universal policies. They are not the best option for most people even though agents will convince you that you'll build all this value and the premiums will magically go away. It's a game, so be careful. Normally, it's best to keep your investments and your insurance separate.

Many employers offer some life insurance protection. Take it, but don't stop there. You may end up changing jobs, and you don't want to get caught without coverage. Keep a policy or two independent from your job.

Finally, know that the goal is to become self-insured. That means you've read the previous chapters and have followed our advice. You've saved. You've invested. If lightning strikes you down tomorrow, your family will have enough to replace your lost income. No, they can't replace you, but financially speaking, they'll be fine. That's when you are free to drop those insurance policies.

Loss of Property: Car, Home, Etc.

Cars, homes, furnishings... all can be covered by some form of property insurance. Rules for all:

- Shop around.

- Read the fine print and ask questions if you need to.

- Build a good relationship with your local agent. You'll need her when that roof caves in.

- Regularly review your policy.

Loss of Health: Health Insurance

Most developed countries have health insurance through some form of government program. In the US, we do it differently, in that most of us get our health insurance through our employer. There's a reason for that, so a little history.

During WWII, the country was experiencing inflation, so the government decided to freeze wages to help control prices. The problem is that this coincided with our entry into and ramp up for fighting alongside the Allies in the Great War.

Manufacturing companies were quickly building ships, planes and munitions, and they needed workers. Many of the young men were heading overseas to do the actual fighting, so this is where a lot of women started entering the workforce. Thank goodness for Rosie the Riveter!

But in the middle of a labor crunch with frozen wages, employers were left with a conundrum. How do we get the employees we need to keep producing the things needed in the war effort? How do we keep up with demand in a tight labor force? Normally, the answer is in offering higher wages. With that option off the table, employers went in another direction. They decided to "pay" employees more without officially calling it "pay." That means a benefits package. At that point, offering employees health insurance was a way to get them to sign on. And even when wages got "unfrozen," the system stuck.

When you go in for a job interview, this is an important topic of conversation. For most employers, health insurance coverage is expected by the employees. Only companies with lower-end service employees tend to avoid this expense. Older people have the advantage of actual government-sponsored healthcare when they hit age 65, which is when you qualify for Medicare. Mark the calendar! What a relief that will be. Millions of Americans get their health insurance through this system.

MedicAID is the government insurance program for lower income people. About 76 million people are in this program. With the introduction of Obamacare, another 11 million got coverage through the exchanges. Still, there are those with no insurance at all—something that would strike fear in our hearts, especially as we age and things start falling apart. Currently, about 155 million of us get our health insurance through our employer. So, employer-provided insurance is still an American thing.

If you're young, you may wonder why you need health insurance at all. Isn't it like buying life insurance on children? Well, not quite. While it's true that young people don't get sick as often and if they do it's usually something minor, there are still high risks to suffering a big health event. Nancy's first husband died of cancer at the tender age of 34. The health insurance he had through his employer saved them. Without it, they would have ended up bankrupt. How would Nancy have crawled out of that financial hole after his death?

Young people can end up in an accident: car accidents, work-related accidents or just stupid-choices accidents. Those accidents can result in catastrophic events and catastrophic expenses. Some young people think it's wiser to pay the penalty for NO health insurance than to pay the monthly premium for coverage. Again, crazy! You're rolling the dice, and snake-eyes can end up costing not just you, but your entire family—because Mom and Dad are unlikely to just let you die on the side of the road. They will do everything they can to keep their sweet baby alive and well, and it just might bankrupt THEM in the process. So protect yourself. Protect your family. Do the right thing. GET INSURANCE!

But why is our system that relies on employers for coverage an economic problem? Because people are making decisions about where they will work, who they will work for and how long they will work based only on health insurance. Now, that's crazy! Want to start a business when you're 35 and, hopefully, end up creating wealth and jobs? Oh, but you have three growing kids and can't take the chance of going without health insurance. Want to retire early and do something totally different like be a tour guide on a train? Oh, but you won't have health insurance. Want to retire and go home before age 65 so that younger workers can take your place? Sorry, you won't have health insurance.

Health insurance, or the lack thereof, is driving our economic decisions. We can't choose the best path for ourselves when this is hanging over our heads. And what about the employers facing rising costs as they continue to offer the expected health insurance? They're screaming for help.

Corporations should not be in the business of health insurance (unless they are actual health insurance companies). They should not be spending time and money trying to keep their employees satisfied with decent coverage. They, too, are making economic decisions based on health insurance.

But this is the system we're left with, and until it changes, you need to understand what your employer is offering. After all, this is really just another part of your pay package. But it's a critical part, especially if you find yourself in critical condition.

Know what your plan covers. Obamacare introduced certain requirements for health insurance policies. Before, companies could sell ANY plan as health insurance, even if the coverage was skimpy and the deductibles were high. Many have been fooled into thinking they have good health insurance until they get sick. Then they realize their plan isn't worth the paper it's written on.

Now, these rules may change, but creating standard policies gives US protection from shady insurance companies. They also give us protection against employers looking for a cheap alternative to coverage. While you may not use all of the things on that list, it's a reasonable list. And as you age, you'll come to appreciate the broader coverage.

Does your employer pay the entire premium for you? Most do, but some have a cost-sharing arrangement. That means less on your paycheck. Does your employer cover your family? Most don't. So if you have a stay-at-home spouse and children, expect to pay a hefty premium to give them the same coverage. For two-earner families with children, it's important to figure out the best option to cover the kids. Which worker's insurance will be the best for family coverage?

Are there certain doctors or hospitals you have to use? Typically, companies have arrangements with these healthcare providers, which allows them to pay a lower fee for service. The lists will be online somewhere. Find them!

Some will participate in an HMO or PPO. What are these? HMO stands for Health Maintenance Organization, and PPO stands for Preferred Provider Organization. Both offer financial benefits to you for using their system of doctors, clinics and hospitals. Usually, that doesn't mean you CAN'T go to someone else, but it will cost you more if you do.

If you need to "go out of network," you need to do it through a referral from a doctor that is IN the network. This is common with serious or rare illnesses. Also, if you're traveling, there are exceptions to using their list of doctors. In fact, Nancy has a special insurance card that she uses when she travels. Of course, if she breaks a leg in London, they'll pick up the tab. It seems they want the tourists happy and healthy.

Sometimes, more important than the doctors and clinics is the drug coverage. Know what drugs your plans will cover. WARNING! It's complicated with different tiers and differences between generic and brand name, but dive in anyway. Oftentimes, you can enter your specific prescriptions into a search feature on the insurer's website to find a plan that best covers you. Many people have medications they take on a regular basis, so this can be a big deal. If you must, call the insurance administrator. Have a conference with your pharmacist. Both may take up a significant part of an otherwise lovely day, but it's worth it!

Typically, insurance policies have a deductible. It's a certain amount of money that YOU must spend before the insurance company begins picking up the tab. Know this only applies to what they COVER, so make sure you get that one down first. These are calculated by calendar year. Every January 1st, your deductible calculator starts over. It's the reason your medicine costs more in January than in November.

As you hit the end of the year, make use of the deductible. You should be able to monitor online what this amount is. Schedule those end-of-year doctor visits. Get all your meds renewed. Once the ball drops in Times Square, it's back to square one.

Even if you hit the deductible, you'll find yourself still paying a little something on most things. That's called the co-pay. Make sure you understand what that will be each time you check in at the doctor. You don't want to face a surprise at the check-out desk at the same time you're dealing with a raging case of poison ivy.

So, ask about the insurance plan of your employer. Know what it covers and who it covers. If they don't offer a plan, take a look at the Obamacare exchanges. (It doesn't matter if you like Obama or not, you still need coverage.) Finally, pay attention to what Congress is doing. This is a big issue, and you can expect changes during your lifetime. Those policy changes will have a drastic effect on your health and your pocketbook. Make sure your voice is heard.

Loss of Health: Dental Insurance

Dental expenses can be huge, and we don't think about them as much as other health problems. 42% of people don't have any dental insurance at all. Those twice a year cleanings can be quite manageable; it's not that expensive. But when you get into cavities and crowns and veneers, they can be very expensive and very difficult to manage. We can tell you from personal experience that dental costs rise with age. You start to have all kinds of problems with your teeth, and they're expensive problems.

A quarter of people over 65 don't have any teeth at all. So, now we're talking prosthetics and all of the things that entails. It can be very, very expensive.

Dental insurance can be a misnomer. What we find is there are very low deductibles, very limited on your coverage. Usually, it's just for the cleanings—those twice a year cleanings. In fact, the insurance companies count on us not going for our twice a year checkups so that they make money off of us. Basically, dental insurance is just like prepaid dental plans, because you just get back the benefit cost.

If your employer is covering dental insurance, then great. You need to make sure you use it twice a year. But if it's an optional plan, I would think twice about signing up for it. You have other options.

You might want to look at an actual dental plan. There are membership plans out there, and you pay a membership fee. You can find out if your dentist participates and compare plans. You can go to brighter.com (that is an actual plan). Plug in your ZIP code and find dentists in your area who participate. You can go to dentalplans.com, a site that allows you to search many different types of plans to see what fits your needs. You'll likely find savings in the range of 20-50% on those participating dentists. That really is a better deal than paying for that dental insurance out of pocket yourself.

Loss of Health: Long-Term Care Insurance

If you're young, long-term care insurance is probably not on your radar, but talk to your parents about it. We're living longer and facing chronic illnesses as we age. Long-term care insurance helps cover the expenses if we end up needing help at home or even if we need to go to a facility.

Medicaid covers long-term care for lower-income people. While about 40% of Medicaid is paid out to nursing homes, don't count on this. Many facilities won't accept Medicaid. It pays to make sure you can cover your own expenses if this situation arises. You do this by either accumulating enough in savings to pay for it yourself, or you buy a long-term care policy.

If your parents think this might be a good choice for them, tell them to start talking to agents when they are in their 50s. Delaying results in higher premiums. Many people wait until their 70s to think about this. It's usually too late then. Get quotes from two to three companies. Ask for an inflation rider. Make sure the insurance company is financially sound by checking with your state insurance commissioner. Then, make a choice based on the premium.

Entire families can be devastated by the costs associated with long-term care of a family member. We're all going to face the inevitable and most will face it after a long illness or period of decline. Make sure you've covered the biggest "what if" of them all.

Annual Insurance Review

Finally, don't just purchase insurance policies, lock them in the safety deposit box, and then forget about them. Things change. Once a year, pull out those policies and take a look at them. List the company and the policy number. Check the name on the policy and contact information, because you want to be able to get your hands on this information when you need it. Keep all of your policies in a safe place. Let a trusted family member or friend know where they are. Of course, you can also put them in a computer file so someone can get to them, or you can list them in your phone.

Most of the time when we talk to people, the biggest problem we see is they have too much insurance. We have to balance protecting ourselves with not getting carried away. If we do, it can end up costing too much and hurting our other finances. You want to make sure all your bases are covered, but you don't need to double up or triple up.

Concerning instances where people have too much insurance, often they will double up on health insurance. I see cancer policies on top of other policies even though the other insurance policies will cover cancer. Many times you have people who will still hang on to life insurance policies even though they've built up enough assets and their children are grown and don't depend on them financially anymore. We'll see whole life or universal life insurance policies whose cash balances are declining with age. That's when it's time to cancel the policy, take the cash and run.

With each policy, ask: Would this money be better spent somewhere else (investing it, for instance)?

Start with your homeowners policy. Make sure that the policy is big enough to cover replacement of your home. Remember that the value of your home changes with time.

With your life insurance policy, make sure there are people who are dependent on your income, because that's when you need to keep life insurance. Life changes, such as a marriage, a divorce, a birth, a death, etc. are times to review these policies. Review the beneficiaries periodically and update them promptly. At some point when you get older, you may build up enough in assets that you no longer need life insurance.

Health insurance is extremely important. Keep a list of preferred providers. Understand your coverage. For most, you should forget dental insurance.

Disability insurance may be appropriate for you. Many employers will offer disability coverage, so check with them to see if that's available. Have a plan in place for how you will be able to deal with disability if it happens to you. It's much easier to handle such an event if you've already planned for it.

Concerning car insurance—compare those costs. It's a highly competitive marketplace.

Finally, make sure other family members are protected, because you may find yourself supporting their care. At the very least, there will be less to pass on to heirs if your parents end up spending down your inheritance.

Insurance is a big expense for many people. Make sure you're getting your money's worth.

As a Wise P.I.G.G.Y. Once Said:

- Only get insurance for the big "what ifs."

- Don't buy insurance policies for children.

- Disability insurance is just as important as life insurance.

- It doesn't matter how old you are, health insurance is CRITICAL! Get it. Get it from your employer. Get it from the exchanges. Get it from the government. Just GET IT!

- Forget dental insurance. It's usually not worth it.

- Understand EVERY policy you have—what it covers, what it costs.

- Shop around for coverage on property insurance.

- Review all policies annually and pay attention to policy changes.

- Call or write your congressmen/women. March in the streets if you must. Insurance is a BIG deal.

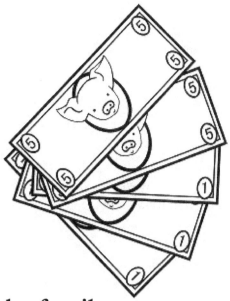

Keep it in the family.

Relationships and Money

You and your better half look great in pictures, but what does your combined financial picture look like?

We've heard stories of people bringing up finances on a first date, or even in a Tinder profile; but, generally speaking, the people who do that are monumental jerks bragging about how much they make (read: exaggerating). The first date is probably a little too soon. On the flip side, we've heard of people finding out about significant debts only after the marriage ceremony. If you're trying to figure out an appropriate time to bring up finances, try some time in between those two examples.

In all seriousness, money is an important topic and is the cause of many break-ups. You need to make sure that you can link your financial lives without someone committing murder. When you first start dating, there may be some pressure to make a date particularly nice. If your taste falls either more expensive or more frugal than your partner appears, bring it up! Tell them that you appreciate the steak and wine for dinner, but you don't mind a modest night in with takeout and the latest Netflix original. If you're tired of peanut butter sandwich picnics in the park, propose something more your style. This can get the conversation started about expectations on spending.

Your first big trip or project together will be a big expense, too. Absolutely talk about how you will pay for it and how you will approach paying for it later. If it's clear that one partner makes the bulk of the money, understand what that money pays for and what it doesn't. Discuss how you expect large expenses to play out in the future.

For a more precise time to talk about things like income and retirement savings, try April 15th. We only slightly kid here. April 15th is when taxes are due, so the topic is fairly natural then. If you've started talking about the future, it's appropriate to start discussing how to pay for that future.

Managing money as a couple starts with looking to see where your goals and values agree and where they don't. When you share finances, it's important that your large, long-term priorities align. This is reasonably important as a couple, but you're not here for relationship coaching. When it comes to meeting large, long-term financial goals, you need all the help you can get, and your partner will be just as important as you in meeting them.

What Are Our Shared Goals and Values?

If finances have come up in your relationship, other goals and values probably have as well. Do you love to travel? That costs money. Do you have your eye on a house in the suburbs and 2.8 children going to your alma mater? You're going to have to pay for that somehow. Do you want to live in a van, travel the world and live a minimalist lifestyle? That is probably inexpensive but definitely will involve financial decisions. As a couple, figure out what you value enough to make you spend your hard-earned money. What do you value enough of your partner's goals to spend money on? And what do you want to spend their money on?

A saver can get along with a spender, but you need to be clear about your limits. In every couple, there is that one person. You know her. The saver. The frugal one. The ultra-responsible one. Then, there's the other one—carefree, a spendthrift. Can it really work?

A saver may not want to subsidize the spender too much, but as a couple you will be spending on each other to some extent. And as a couple with shared goals and expenses, you will need to compromise if your habits are wildly different.

It's rare to find a couple with partners earning the same amount. There even may be times when only one partner is working, while the other has no income. That disparity in income can sometimes lead to tension. Having common goals will help. They remind you that it's not "yours" or "mine" but "ours." You are working together.

Even if you understand that, it's often a good plan to have a little freedom in your spending. This can happen with separate bank accounts, or it can happen by agreeing to certain spending limits without the other person passing judgment.

When it comes to couples and money, we say: Whatever works. For some, that means keeping everything totally separate. For others, it means putting it all together. One way or another, the bills have to be paid. Taxes have to be paid. And saving has to happen. If you can keep talking and always come back to the same financial goals, you should be able to stay on track.

In a couple, one person is usually better at handling money than the other. Regardless of who does what, it's important that everybody knows what's going on. No matter how little you think you know about finance or how much you trust your partner to handle it, it's very important that each partner keep informed of the couple's finances. Retirement accounts are an important part of this, but a savings or taxable investment account that is your own is also important for the unknown. This is not about keeping money hidden from your partner, but about ensuring that you can stand on your own if an expense arises.

Whoever handles more of the day-to-day financial responsibility should also be responsible for keeping the other partner informed of the couple's financial situation. Far too often we've seen recently widowed or separated partners overwhelmed with the mass of new information. We've seen people get taken advantage of or simply make sub-optimal choices because they didn't know what all they had and could do with their finances. Each partner should know what regular expenses you share, how much they are and how they are paid. Each partner should know what assets and debts the couple and the other partner have. While you may not have access to each other's accounts, it is important to know what the account is for and what will happen to it if the other partner dies.

Where Exactly Does This Money Go?

The technical aspects of how your money will flow through accounts and who will own what should depend on how your values and goals align. There are three basic options for how you handle joint finances:

1. Each person has individual taxable accounts and his or her own money, and every expense is handled according to some predetermined rule or ad hoc agreement.

2. The couple shares everything in a jointly owned account.

3. A little of both.

*Note that retirement accounts are always in each individual's name.

First, every couple needs to understand their shared expenses and agree on a clear and fair plan for paying them. The technical workings of this will depend on what makes sense to you, but one way would be to have a joint checking account that you each contribute to. Each partner contributes his or her share on a regular basis. Another method is just assigning different expenses to one another. If this is the route you take, keep in mind that expenses can change, so it's fair to take a look at these on a regular basis to make sure each partner is happy with what they are paying.

With regular expenses, it's very important that communication be open, honest and frequent. Since most expenses occur on a monthly basis, take the time to go over expenses and contributions at least that often. This is a good time to make sure that you are still on budget and to talk about any financial issues that have come up.

There is no right or wrong way to determine a fair contribution. If one partner makes substantially all of the money, it may make sense for them to contribute most or all of the money for expenses. If incomes are roughly equal, an even split makes sense. Determine what works for you. In general, the higher your income is above your joint expenses, the less the split matters. For example, if your joint expenses are $2,000 per month and each partner makes $1,000 per month, there aren't many ways to make that split. But for the same level of expense and each partner making $10,000 per month, neither may care that much exactly how much they have to contribute. For meaningful, but unequal incomes, a fair method may be to do a rough ratio. If one partner makes $10,000 per month and the other makes $4,500 per month, the partner with the lower income could contribute one third and the partner with the larger income could contribute two thirds of their joint expenses. It doesn't have to be difficult or terribly precise just so long as each partner is understanding and happy with the outcome.

Keep in mind that retirement accounts are only owned by a single person, so each of you should max these out to the extent that you can. These accounts will depend partly on what is available to you at your job, so you may not have a lot of control over it. In the case of drastically different incomes, it may make sense for the spouse with the higher income to contribute more to regular expenses to allow the other partner to contribute more to his or her retirement plan. Outside of work retirement plans, you should max out personal retirement accounts if possible. This is an important part of the money that is individually owned.

While retirement accounts can only be registered to ONE person, bear in mind that your retirement will still be a joint adventure—assuming you're still together when that happens. But that doesn't mean you should fund only ONE person's retirement expecting it to cover you both. It's important that both partners save for this event. It may not be equal savings, but you still need to have your own set of retirement accounts.

It wasn't so long ago that the traditional family ruled. Dad worked and earned. Mom stayed at home. Not so much anymore. In 40% of households, women earn more than their male partners. Even when a partner stops earning, they should still be saving for retirement. In fact, it may be more important, since they aren't building earnings through Social Security. Spousal IRAs allow non-working spouses to contribute to their own retirement accounts even if they have no earnings. Check with your CPA.

If your financial values are quite different, it will be important for you to have your own money. It's difficult to have two people sharing an account if they view it completely differently! Keeping it separate may be the only way to keep the peace. In this case, money that you save beyond regular expenses, shared goals and retirement accounts should be kept in individually owned accounts. This can be savings or investments. With different values, each partner can treat his or her money differently; one may choose to spend and the other to save.

Keeping separate accounts requires a bit of trust. Is your partner really paying those bills? Are they building up credit card debt without your knowledge? Quarterly financial meetings between you should help. Pull out the bank statements and bills and open a bottle of wine. This can be quite romantic!

If you still can't agree, that's where we come in. An objective, knowledgeable third party may be the way to go. That person should listen to both of you attentively, then make recommendations to help you meet your goals. You should leave the office with a roadmap and, hopefully, some peace of mind. Be prepared, though. We often have a frugal partner who wants us to gang up on their spendthrift spouse. It doesn't always work out that way. If you get professional help, you both need to agree to be honest, to listen to the advice and to commit to a plan together.

How Does This All Come Together?

There is no one perfect way to manage your personal finances, and there are plenty more ways to manage finances as a couple. The important thing is that you find a method that works for you. If something isn't working correctly, have an open and honest conversation about it. Just because you decide to keep some things separate doesn't mean you have to keep them hidden.

If your financial values are very well aligned, it may make sense to simplify things with a joint account for the bulk of the rest of your money. The more aligned goals are, the more you can share actual ownership of money. Decide on what is personal and what is private. Understand that it's fine for either partner to have money that they have unfettered access to. This doesn't mean you must keep your spending private – just that you have an account you can spend from without your partner's permission or judgment. Sometimes that means an account that is totally separate. Sometimes that means settling on an amount above which you check in with your partner. Honesty and transparency are often good for relationships, but again, our advice is about money.

However you decide to manage money together, open communication is paramount. You both need to be clear about what your income and expenses are now and how you expect those to change in the future. While you don't have to contribute to every financial goal your partner may have, it is important that you share what those goals are so you can support each other along the way. If you have any debts that may affect your partner, let them know and have a clear discussion about how you plan to deal with them. Financial management is an ongoing responsibility. Have a regular date set up to review your situation and talk about major changes as they arise.

As a couple, you need to figure out your goals and your values, decide on an approach to your finances and keep each other informed along your journey. If you think you can keep your financial lives separate and secret without this conversation, good luck to you. You might want to keep an attorney on retainer, though.

What About the Kids?

Those little creatures are expensive. Diapers. Daycare. Birthday parties. Soccer practice. New shoes. Cell phone. Prom. A car. And the biggest hit of all—college.

Handling the day-to-day expenses will be part of your budget process. Certainly, before you think about procreating, you need to take a look at your budget. But, don't look too hard. If you get obsessed with covering every possible expense, you'll never have a child, and your mother will stop speaking to you. After all, she wants grandchildren.

But, be reasonable. How will you handle childcare? Will one partner stop working to be the caretaker? If so, can you live off one income? If both keep working, what will be the cost of childcare? That depends on where you live and the particular type of childcare you've chosen. Expect to spend somewhere around 10% of your income for this purpose.

That doesn't cover the additional expenses that come with that little human. Add it all up, and you can see just how expensive it is to raise a child. It's the reason so many young parents are under incredible stress. It's enough dealing with no sleep, projectile vomiting and noncompliant little beings under your roof. Add in the financial pressures, and it's no wonder families are barely holding it together.

Our advice to couples considering an addition to the family? Decide what lifestyle you want. Then, begin living within the budget you'll have to keep when Junior comes along. It won't be such a shock when you bring that baby home. Other than that, just hang on! It just might be the scariest, most nausea-inducing, most joyous thing you can ever do.

Don't worry. You'll survive. You'll manage. Those children will grow up. And they'll move away. And not call. And not come see you. And you'll be ready to cut them out of your will until…

They give you grandchildren!

Back to that big expense—college. When should you start preparing? On the way home from the hospital. No, seriously. The sooner the better when it comes to covering a college education, and there are a few special accounts for just that purpose:

- UGMA/UTMA

- State-sponsored plans

- Coverdell

UGMA/UTMA

The UGMA/UTMA accounts are some of the first used for college savings. We have some of these old accounts still out there, but not many. The letters stand for Uniform Gift to Minors Act or Uniform Transfer to Minors Act. Long before we had the special education accounts that we have now, these were used—mainly by grandparents—and their intention was to use that money for education. The problem is that there are very few limits on how that money can actually be spent.

You're going to have two people on these accounts. One will be the custodian. This is the signer, or the adult, on the account. They're allowed to use the money only FOR the minor. Again, this is usually a parent or a grandparent. The money does not belong to the custodian. That's very important. Once the money goes into the account, it belongs to the child and can only be used for and by the child.

What happens when that child becomes an adult? In Mississippi, that age is 21. Officially, then, (legally) that money belongs to the child—to the beneficiary. The beneficiary will need to open a new account and the custodian will need to turn those funds over to the grown child.

What we see happening, though, is many of these custodians just don't tell the beneficiaries about the account and its purpose until the child is an adult. That's really not appropriate, because what happens when that money goes to those adults now who were children? They can spend the money as they please. Many times it was intended for education, but suddenly the child is free to blow it all, and the custodian has no control. But, that's the way the law works.

How do you prepare for that loss of control? Try to use up as much of that money as possible before they reach adulthood. And begin early by teaching them about financial management.

State-Sponsored Plans

These days, we have better options for saving for college. These new accounts put limitations on how the money can be spent and gives some control to the donor. Two types are state-sponsored plans, and here in Mississippi, we offer both.

The first is called MPACT (Mississippi Prepaid Affordable College Trust) and acts like an insurance policy for college. You can buy any number of years and any combination from the state. The cost is based on the options you choose and the age of the child when the purchase is made. You can buy two years at a community college and two years at a university. Or you can buy all four years at a university level. Or, you can buy just one year to help get that child started. It's up to the purchaser.

MPACT only covers tuition, and any parent who has ever sent that child to college knows that's only about half of the cost involved. They need a place to live, a meal plan while at college, textbooks, a computer, any number of additional fees... It all adds up. That's where 529 plans come in.

529 refers to the code in federal law that allows each state to create a college savings plan. Mississippi's 529 plan is called MACS (Mississippi Affordable College Savings). While MPACT is like an insurance policy, MACS is like a 401(k).

There are no standard buy-ins like MPACT. You decide what to contribute (within annual maximums), and you decide how to invest the money. Currently, these match the annual gift tax exclusion of $14,000 per person, but you can combine five years in one contribution with $70,000. Like a 401(k), you'll have a list of funds to choose from. A good choice is the one based on the child's age. It works like the LifeCycle funds for 401(k)s. Younger children are in more aggressive stocks. As the child ages and gets closer to college age, the fund gets more conservative.

The beauty of 529 plans is that they can be used for anything related to the education of that child. They also have a longer life, allowing for graduate school. But they still have to be used for education. With the changes in the tax law, depending on your state, you can use this money for K-12 expenses.

Many state plans offer a tax break, making choosing YOUR state's plan a no-brainer. Make sure the tax break is valuable, though. For grandparents in low income tax brackets, it may be better to look at another state that has access to better funds with lower annual expenses. New York uses Vanguard for their 529 and is a good option if you don't need the tax break. For any of these plans, growth is tax-free, and withdrawals are tax-free, as long as they are used for education.

Finally, there is some confusion about these plans. Many people think that using a state-sponsored plan locks in your child to THAT state's public colleges. Not so! Both plans can be used to pay for college at a private university or an out-of-state school. There are a few qualifiers, but it still works great. Nancy should know! She used MPACT for her daughter who did not attend a public school in her state.

Start by searching for plans offered by the state in which you are a resident. Grandparents who live in a different state may use their own state's plan just to get the tax break. That's perfectly okay. Websites on the plans usually have a FAQ section. Read it! Understand how these work. Know how flexible or limiting they may be before you commit. And, many will allow you to complete forms online to get started for that little one.

Coverdell

The last official education account available is the Coverdell. There are listed income limits for contributors. Look on irs.gov as these change periodically. There is an annual maximum contribution of $2,000 (much lower than the 529). Money in these accounts is not limited to higher education. They can be used for K-12 expenses, so if you have a child in private school, this is a way to invest for that purpose while saving a little on taxes.

IRA Exceptions

Finally, Congress gave us one thing that allows us to avoid the question: Do I save for college, or do I save for my retirement? Traditional and Roth IRAs allow distributions without penalty for educational expenses. If you can't do both (save for retirement and college), sock the money in your own IRA. You'll be able to access it for your child's college. Also, the money in your IRA doesn't count against them as much when they apply for financial aid.

So, get started saving for college while your kids are still in diapers. The cost of a college education keeps going up, and the gift of a debt-free education is invaluable. Encourage family members to create their own college savings accounts or add to ones you have already created. It's better than another toy that will end up on the trash heap in a few months. And, grandparents LOVE to do this! Because now that you have a child, they like those children more than they like you. In fact, don't expect them to even notice you're in the room when that sweet baby is cooing at them.

Keep it in the family.

When Should You Get a Will?

Everyone needs a will. We don't like to think about our eventual deaths, but we all need to address the elephant in the room. If we don't set out what our wishes are before the end, then what we leave behind will pass by state law, and that may not be how you want your legacy disbursed.

Creating a will is really a simple thing to do in the state of Mississippi. It's actually legal if you write it out by hand and sign it at the bottom. Do a little extra and have a neighbor witness it. Keep it in a safe place.

You can also access online services that will help you set up a will based on your state. Again, it's all by state law. We prefer talking to a local attorney, because often when you sit down with one, the attorney will then ask the questions that you have not thought about—about exactly how you want your estate to be divided up. They'll talk to you about your particular family situation.

You need to be explicit in your will and say: This is what I want to happen after I die. You don't want a vague will that could lead to different interpretations of your wishes. It's very important that you name an executor. This is the person who will actually be in charge of making sure all the bills are paid, making sure that everything is distributed based on your will. This needs to be someone you can truly trust. It's extremely important to have a will if you have children, because you'll need to name an official guardian for your kids.

Know that joint accounts do not go through your will. If something happens to you, your spouse will automatically take over that joint account. Also, any accounts that have beneficiaries will not go through the will. That means your 401(k), IRAs and annuities. But, you still need a will. What about that car? Or that piece of land your aunt gave you? Or that separate bank account? Those are the things covered by your will.

You need to update a list of your accounts at least once a year. Keep a list of account numbers and contact information. Be sure to keep it in a safe place. You can hand a copy to your executor or email them a secure copy so that they have it on file in case you die.

Keep copies of all your beneficiary forms, and check these once a year. Things change. Your accounts will be divided up based on that beneficiary form. Insurance policies, retirement accounts, IRAs, 401(k)s and those accounts we call TODs or PODs, meaning Transfer on Death or Pass on Death. Those are legal in the state of Mississippi. These mean that you can take an account and put a beneficiary on that account so that it does not go through the will. It's a faster way for your heirs to inherit those assets.

In order to specify what you want to have happen in terms of life support or feeding tubes, you need a medical power of attorney. Most of these are pretty boiler plate. If you need to, you can sit down with a local attorney for guidance. The paperwork—for most states available online for free— is mostly a series of boxes you check to indicate which option you'd want to have happen in various medical situations. You can specify whether or not you want continuous resuscitation, whether or not you want pain medicine, whether or not you want to donate any of your organs and which ones, whether you want burial, cremation or donation. By taking the time beforehand to make these decisions for yourself, you relieve your loved ones of the burden of having to make these difficult decisions for you. Be sure to give copies of your medical power of attorney to anyone relevant.

With all of these documents, you need to make sure you keep them in a very safe place: a safe deposit box or a fireproof box in your house. Digital copies are also a good idea. Again, that named executor needs to know where they are, and they need to have a key so they can get to all that material. Make copies and give them to your CPA and financial advisor.

While we all hope to live to a ripe old age, there is no guarantee. Your wills and updated beneficiary forms make it easier on your family when your number comes up. These forms spell out who gets your assets. They indicate who is in charge of your estate. And they specify who will take care of your children and their inherited assets.

What about Your Parents?

If you have aging parents, it may be time to check with them about their own state of affairs. Every family is different. Some are quite open in sharing financial information. Others fiercely protect their privacy. Have those conversations. Have them often. And, keep in mind, you too will one day be having these conversations with your own grown children (or whomever you entrust with this responsibility: a niece, a nephew, a trusted friend).

This is a touchy subject to approach. We're talking about money, and many families are very secretive when it comes to the topic. Families fight about it. Siblings get into battles over how it should be handled. Even so, parents need to talk to their grown children. Your children need to know where everything is in case something happens to you. At least make a list of all of those accounts and their balances. You may pass on to them the actual list, or you may simply tell them where they can find it. Keep it in a safe place. That means it needs to be in a lockbox or in a fire safe box. You can keep it online as long as it's stored securely. Let your grown children know where to look if they need to find that information. Update that list once a year. Look it over for your own benefit and for your kids' benefit as well.

Make a list of professionals. Maybe even just get your professionals' cards (attorneys, financial advisors, CPAs), and pass that on to your grown children. Again, this is to give them a person to reach out to, someone to call in case something comes up. And they need to be able to find those wills and powers of attorney. Where are you going to put those papers? Again, in a very safe place. And you need to think very carefully about who will be the executor of the will and who's going to serve as your power of attorney. Talk to that person. Make sure that they're willing to take that on, because it's a tough job. They're going to have to deal with other siblings and all of those issues of settling your estate that may pop up.

Let your family know what's in your will. Don't surprise them with anything. That can be an awful situation. More importantly, you need to give someone your power of attorney. Many financial institutions, like banks, no longer accept outside paperwork for this power. Instead, you have to complete that bank's POA paperwork. It may seem like you're doubling up, but take the time while you still have all your faculties to complete the necessary paperwork. Understand that you're more likely to become disabled and unable to take care of all of your bills on your own. To have someone who can come in and sign for you is wonderful. Of course, you want to be absolutely sure this person can be entrusted with this responsibility and won't abuse the power or neglect the duty. And be careful about putting only some of your children's names on your bank account. This can affect inheritance and cause arguments once you're gone.

You need to talk to those grown children about what your provisions are for retirement and old age. You can gradually let them know about any pensions, tell them your Social Security payment, and talk to them about any long-term care insurance and what that policy will cover. They need to understand what their obligations will be and where they can turn for resources. By the time you need all of those things like long-term care, you may not be in your right mind and able to make those key decisions on your own or to communicate the important details of your finances.

We often talk to older people about this idea of inheritance or of assisting your grown children. It's the most natural thing for us to do as parents: to help our children. We still want to give to them. We sacrifice. But we always say: Take care of yourself first! That's the greatest gift you can give your grown children. If you make sure you can provide for yourself in retirement and old age, then your children won't have to. And if you want to help them, that's fine. Make sure you have the means to do it, but don't enable them. Set some expectations about what you'll pay for and what you won't pay for. It could be something as simple as funding college savings accounts for their children or assisting with the purchase of a home.

Be open with your family members. Don't encourage false expectations. The toughest thing that we hear from parents is how to be fair. You have children with different abilities and resources. It's important to most parents to make sure that whatever they do for one, they do for all of their children.

Caregiving

When it comes to caring for aging parents, most of us will face this in the 50 to 60 age range. The time period we encounter this is critical, because these are our highest income years.

We know a third of us will leave the workforce or reduce our hours to assume the role of primary caregiver. While this is an admirable task to take on, you need to think very carefully about whether or not this is right for you. You are going to be doing some damage to your Social Security. It also means you may not be saving enough for retirement because you aren't able to set aside as much during this period. Consider a consultation with a financial advisor to look at the numbers and to help you navigate the logistics of such a decision.

Start by talking to your existing employer, because many employers offer some sort of assistance. They may offer flexibility in your work hours, and some of them even offer benefits for caregivers. Before you decide to step out of the workforce completely, do your homework with your employer.

We also have the Family and Medical Leave Act. Any employer that has 50 or more employees is required to give you twelve weeks of unpaid leave. Now, remember that this is unpaid, but this rule allows you to then step back into the workforce after time spent caregiving.

If you have a small employer that you're working for, they can often be more flexible, especially if you've been a good employee and have been around for a while. Your value as a skilled and reliable part of the business isn't something to dismiss out of hand.

There are resources available online to help you understand how to care for your family. One website is www.caremanager.org, where you can find someone to help you navigate all of the plans out there and help you figure out what to do in your situation. The government offers assistance as well (www.eldercare.gov). There's another site, www.benefitscheckup.org, which offers assistance on things like pharmaceuticals and specific types of care.

It happens very quickly. Your parents are doing very well; they're independent. Then, suddenly, one crisis can cause them to depend on you, and you need to be prepared to step into that role and to understand how best to provide care for the family unit.

As a Wise P.I.G.G.Y. Once Said:

- Talk about money before the romantic merger.

- As a couple, decide how you will split financial responsibilities.

- Talk, talk, and talk some more about money, accounts and financial goals.

- Get objective help if you hit a crossroads.

- Start saving for college the day you bring a child home from the hospital.

- Use tax-favored plans to save for education.

- Get a will!

- Talk to your parents about their finances and plans.

- Prepare to be a caregiver to aging family members.

- When it comes to money and family, expect the discussions to be difficult.

Stay informed.

Economics

If you want to understand finance and the world of investing, you have to know a little something about economics. MACROeconomics is the study of the overall economy, the big picture. Companies that are operating in a healthy economy have a better chance of doing well than those in a weak economy.

Economics is all about scarce resources and unlimited wants. We all make choices about our situation based on our limited funds and our really big wish lists.

The overall economy is a bundle of all of these choices each of us is making. The ripple effect of those choices determines if we're in recession or if we're in expansion. That cycle from a growing economy to a shrinking economy is called the business cycle. Basically, it's an ebb and flow—an indicator that we cannot stay perpetually in one state or another.

Where we are in that cycle affects every one of us every day. The driver behind this is the supply and demand for money. Put supply and demand on a graph, and find the cross point. That will be the price of the thing you're graphing. In the case of money, the price is the interest rate; and current interest rates affect every one of us every day.

You need to understand some basic economic concepts and be able to interpret the data we use to measure all aspects of that economy. We can't cover everything you need to know in a few pages, but we'll give you a few lessons on the most important things. We'll also explain some terms to help with investing. Knowing the language is half the battle.

Beyond that, read. Expand your knowledge about economics, and you'll have a great foundation as an investor. Heck, you'll have a great foundation as a consumer!

GDP

GDP stands for Gross Domestic Product. It's a measure of economic activity, and it's like taking the temperature of the economy. We want it to be moving along nicely, but we don't want it to get too overheated.

GDP is measured by quarter. The government has agencies who collect all kinds of statistics on the economy, and GDP is one of these statistics. Normally, if we have two consecutive quarters that are negative, it could signal a recession. These numbers can fluctuate because of all kinds of things, and quarterly numbers are often revised. We eventually look at annual GDP growth and make predictions for future years.

What makes up those numbers? There are four pieces, and we can look down into the data at those four pieces. The first is "G": Government Spending. All kinds of governments spend money, and when they do so, they create positive economic activity. Then, the big "C": Consumer Spending represents about two thirds of economic activity. WE are the most important piece to our economic health. If we are spending money, the world goes round and everybody is happy. Business Spending or

Investment Type Capital Spending is another piece. Of course, businesses don't spend if we (the customers) aren't spending, so it's connected. The final piece is Net Exports. In the US, we import more than we export. That's called a trade deficit. That's not, in and of itself, a bad thing. Understand that America is a wealthy nation full of consumers. We buy what other countries produce, and they don't have as many people who can afford to buy all that stuff. That is changing. The buying and selling of goods across borders (along with many other things) determines the differences in currencies. This has an impact on our trade deficit (and whether we go to England over the summer).

Ultimately, the real driver is consumer spending, so we watch additional pieces of data that tell us about that factor.

Jobs Data

The Bureau of Labor and Statistics (www.bls.gov) tracks jobs numbers. There are many pieces of information that tell us about the health of the job market, but let's take a look at a few.

Weekly Unemployment Claims

Each Thursday, we get data on the number of new people who file unemployment from the week before. Because this is weekly data, it can vary widely, and we can have a weird bad week in the middle of a bunch of good weeks. That makes it important to look at this number over a period of weeks. At the height of the 2008 recession, we saw weekly claims of over 600,000. Anything below 300,000 keeps us moving in the right direction.

Monthly Unemployment Rate

On the first Friday of the month, we get monthly employment data based on the previous month. One piece is the unemployment rate. At the height of the Great Recession, we had an unemployment rate over 10%. We are now under 4.5%. We'll never get to zero, though, because there are always people moving around, changing jobs, entering the workforce, etc. Anything below 5% is excellent. While the official unemployment rate gets the most press, it's not the most reliable. The way this number is calculated leaves a lot of room for fluctuation, so investors prefer the next number we'll look at.

Monthly Jobs Added

This number comes out the first Friday of each month, and this piece of information is produced in such a way that is found to be more reliable. Jobs added is the total of new jobs minus loss of old jobs. We need to produce about 150,000 new jobs each month just to cover new people coming into the job market.

Why are numbers on jobs so important? Well, it's back to consumer spending. If you don't have a job, you're not likely to buy that cute new outfit. Or if you have a job but are worried about layoffs, you won't commit to a new house or a new car. A strong jobs market with opportunities for advancement and higher incomes means we have more resources for that big wish list of ours.

Consumer Sentiment

Consumer sentiment is a fuzzy area. We actually survey households and collect information to produce a number that says how confident we are about the economy. Remember, the economy all boils down to people. How we are feeling about ourselves, our little town and our world determines how active we are economically speaking. Consumer confidence is the grease of our economic engine. It's connected to two other pieces of data: consumer spending and savings rates. It can be affected by all kinds of weird things. Earthquake on the other side of the world? We're fearful and pull in. Gridlock in Congress? Our wallets seize up. Terrorist attack? We sit at home and eat macaroni and cheese. Because the news travels so fast and is so pervasive, we internalize every bit, which is reflected in economic activity. And you thought economics was about accounting and math? No, it's more about psychology.

Interest Rates and Inflation

Remember that supply and demand thing? In financial markets, the "thing" that we're selling is money. People need money to buy cars, to buy houses, to start businesses, to get educations, etc. Where do we get that money? From people with more money than they are using right now.

Who has more money than they need? Investors! The job of financial markets is to match the people with money (savers or investors) with the people who need money. The price of that money is the interest rate. Sometimes we call this the rate of return or the return on investment. It boils down to a number quoted in percentage terms that is on the price tag for that money we just borrowed.

Current market rates are determined by supply and demand. What affects supply and demand? It's the economy, stupid. (No, we're not really trying to offend you, just using an old political phrase.)

When the economy is doing well, more people are willing to borrow money for all kinds of things. Businesses expand. New businesses pop up. We buy houses, cars, appliances and anything else we can get our hands on. We get a new mortgage, apply for a student loan, break out the credit card; and each time, we are buying money in the financial market. Greater demand for money and all the stuff it can buy causes interest rates to go up.

When we are in recession, rates are dropping. We worry about our jobs. We make do with the old car. We pay DOWN our credit card debt. That means the demand for money is declining. We always have these changes in interest rates, but current rates have a drastic impact on our spending ability. Since the Financial Crisis of 2008, interest rates have been historically low. Low rates mean lower house payments, lower car payments, lower cost for everything. As Americans, that means we're buying bigger houses and more expensive cars because it costs less!

When we talk about interest rates, we must bear in mind that there are two numbers in every interest rate figure. There are real rates and nominal rates. The real rate actually doesn't change that much. The nominal rate, though, swings widely and includes inflation. While nominal rates affect our choices on the size of house or the type of car we can afford, real rates drive investor decisions, because inflation is a cost. It affects our ability to purchase things in the future.

The classic definition of inflation is "too much money chasing too few goods." We don't have inflation right now. If you're shopping, you know that. You know you can get a deal on a house, on a car, on clothing—all of those things are on sale. Now, for some of our older clients, they think we have inflation because they're not purchasing those things right now. They're not buying new furniture, new houses, new cars. They're seeing their grocery bills go up, and they think: Oh my goodness, inflation! But we don't currently have those conditions.

Inflation is measured by the government with the CPI, which is the Consumer Price Index. This measures the change in prices in a typical basket of goods that we might buy. There is a little bias in there, because it's only adjusted every two years.

We do know that inflation averages over the long haul at about 3% a year. Inflation is linked to interest rates, so as inflation goes up, interest rates go up. So, be careful what you ask for when you look for higher rates on your CDs. That means all those prices will go higher as well.

High inflation is bad for growth. If it gets too high, then we spend all of our money now, because we know it's not going to be worth as much a year from now.

In conditions with very low or no inflation, your real return is still in the positive territory, and that's a good thing.

We always hear that back in the late 70s and early 80s, we had double digit CD rates. But we had double digit inflation, too. We had 10%, 13%, 14%

inflation. We had mortgage rates that were double-digit, as well. We can't imagine that right now. Just remember: low inflation and low CD rates will go together. Inflation is going to track your interest rates. Concentrate on the real rate of return, which is what you earn after inflation.

Deflation may mean lower prices for goods, but it's not necessarily a good thing, because it can really drag our economy down. We want to have just a little bit of inflation. In most developed economies, there is a central bank that has some control over interest rates and inflation. Ours is called the Federal Reserve Bank.

Federal Reserve

The Federal Reserve Bank was created in 1913 in response to all the booms and busts of the economy. Our business cycles used to resemble the Colorado Rocky Mountains—big upswings to a quick peak, then diving just as quickly to the valley. It was all quite painful.

We knew we couldn't perpetually stay in expansion, but we wanted a mechanism that would help us smooth out the business cycle and ease some of the pain for regular people. Thus, the Federal Reserve was created and given the power to control the supply of money. This is called monetary policy.

When they control the supply of money, they control the price of money. The idea is that if they lower the price of money, we'll buy more; and if they raise the price of money, we'll slow down and buy less. It's not a perfect mechanism, though. In the last crisis, they kept lowering the interest rate but no one was buying. We were still hiding under our desks!

You may have heard of this process as "printing money." Now, they don't actually print it. They create it through a rather strange system called reserve banking. Through this system, they can create or destroy money. By affecting the supply of money in our economy, they have an impact on interest rates. If they put too much money out there, we'll have inflation.

The Gold Standard and the Federal Reserve did function at the same time for a short period of time. The Gold Standard was totally phased out by 1971. With the Gold Standard, gold is pegged to our currency at a fixed price. The good thing about doing that is you end up with low inflation. The bad thing about doing that is you have no mechanism when you use only the Gold Standard to address recessions—to be able to spur on the economy and address high unemployment. That's a problem. People sometimes ask: Can't we go back to the Gold Standard? Well, we don't have enough gold to match the currency that we have out there right now, so that would be very difficult.

The other things we have to look at are the tradeoffs. With the Federal Reserve, we're going to have some inflation because of this printing of money, but we will also have lower unemployment than we would have under the Gold Standard. With the high unemployment that we saw during the Great Recession, if we had not had the Federal Reserve to help us through this crisis, our unemployment would have been even higher.

The Federal Reserve operates in twelve districts that were set based on the population in 1913, and it hasn't changed. Mississippi is in the 6th district. Every district collects economic data, and they act on that data.

There are many other economic statistics out there that tell us about the economy, but the information above will get you started. These stats are like football stats. Each one tells us something different. Each must be considered in light of trends and of the big picture.

Now, let's go on to a few terms and explanations for investors.

What is a Stock?

Stock is an equity obligation or ownership. When you own stock, you are an owner in a company. You are subject to everything that an owner is subject to. You own a share of the future earnings of that company. If the company makes money, then you participate in the gains. If they lose money, then you participate in the losses. That's the way it works. You hope that at some point the company is making enough to give some of those earnings back to their shareholders (you) in the form of dividends. Eventually, when you're ready to sell your shares, you hope that the share price has appreciated because the company has grown and is now worth more than it was when you first invested. If it has, you make money on the terminal side.

How do you buy and sell shares of stock? You have to go through a broker with connections to the formal stock exchanges. You can open an account at TD Ameritrade, E-Trade, Schwab, etc. where you have the ability to place trades. It's as simple as that.

With stock, the hard part is figuring out the best companies to buy. You have to be a bit of a Sherlock Holmes, poring over financial statements and reading between the lines. You also have to be a bit of a fortune teller, predicting the future prospects for a company.

Stay away from hot tips and message boards if you're not willing to combine that with your own due diligence. Investing in the stock market should not be like going to the casino. You're going to be an owner, taking all the risks of ownership but getting all the rewards as well. You need to take a deep dive into the specifics of that business before you pull the lever.

As a stockholder, you are a residual owner. That means if the company gets into trouble, you get whatever is left over after all the bills and creditors have been paid. For many, that means zip, zero. You could lose EVERYTHING you put into the stock.

The good news, though, is that you won't lose more than the price of the stock. Because public corporations are "C" corporations with their own identity and life, you cannot be sued for personal assets. If a pharmaceutical company produces a pill that kills people, shareholders are not personally on the hook. The corporation will be sued, and shareholders may lose the value of their initial investment, but that's the extent of it.

So, a few things about stock ownership…

Dividends

Not all companies pay dividends. These payments come out of a company's earnings, but the managers of the company need to make sure they keep enough on hand to continue growing the business. Fast-growing companies often don't pay out ANY dividends, while slower-growth companies generally pay out some portion of earnings.

Dividends may be paid out in cash or in more shares of stock. Take the cash. Those stock dividends don't mean a thing and are only designed to make you feel better. Pass on these.

Cash dividends come out of the company's accounts or assets, so they reduce the total value of the company. If they reduce the total, expect them to reduce the price per share. The Board of Directors decides on how much of the earnings should be paid out to shareholders. You must own the shares on a specific date to qualify for the dividend. Two days before the dividend is paid out, the shares will trade at a lower price. This is called the ex-dividend date.

Cash dividends are usually paid quarterly and are taxed as investment income. It won't be as high as your income tax bracket, though. If those dividends are in retirement accounts, you don't pay tax on them at all (at least while they stay in the account). Check with your CPA on what to expect.

Companies who give cash to their owners are nice to have in your portfolio. They are usually solid, stable companies with long histories of good earnings. They provide good income to their shareholders, and the tax is often less than your income tax rate.

Stock Split

Everybody gets excited about a stock split, but we're going to explain to you that maybe you shouldn't get quite so riled up. A while back, the big split was Apple stock. It was a 7:1 split, which meant that if you had 100 shares before, you now held 700 shares. Sounds great, except the price adjusts. So, it really doesn't make any difference. Before the split, the price was around $700 a share. After the split, the price was only about $100 a share. You have seven times more shares, but they're only worth a seventh as much, so the value ends up being the same.

This is like that $10 pizza you order. Well, you could slice that pizza into quarters or into eighths, but the value of the whole pizza doesn't change. It's still a $10 pizza. That's the same way when a company splits its stock. It might be a 2:1 split or a 3:1 split. You could even have a reverse split, like a 1:3, meaning if you had 3 shares before, now you only have 1. This is done to get into the sweet spot on the price.

Remember, though, that regardless of the split, the value of the whole company doesn't change. So, why do people get so excited about the split? Well, more investors can now afford to buy a round lot, which is 100 shares. Demand in the short run will push up the price, so in the short run, you will have a bump up in the price. In the long run, remember, it's still a $10 pizza, so splits are not really important to long-term investors.

What about taxes? Well, when it comes to splits, you don't have to pay taxes when the split occurs. Your original cost will adjust to account for that. Other than that, it's just more shares.

Index

A stock index is a measure of how the overall stock market is doing. It is a benchmark, something we can use to compare our investments to. But not every index is created equally.

One of the ones that we hear so much about is the Dow Jones Industrial Average. It's one of the oldest, but it's a very simple index. Although it's popular in the media, the Dow only represents 30 companies—30 big US companies. It started with one share of each of those 30 companies, but it has changed through the years.

A better index to compare your portfolio's performance to would be the S&P 500, because it's made up of 500 large-cap companies and weighted by the size of the company.

The NASDAQ index is made up of all the companies listed on that particular exchange. It's very heavy in technology and in small companies.

The Russell 2000 is made up of more than 2000 stocks and includes large and small companies. This makes it a better measure of overall market movement.

You can buy a fund that tracks an index: a mutual fund or an exchange traded fund (ETF). The index is not one stock or one company but represents a collection of stocks. You get instant diversification with a fund that tracks an index. So, if you're not sure which company's stock to pick, then you can choose to invest in an index.

Countries have their own index that helps to track and measure how the overall market is doing: DAX in Germany, FTSE (Footsie) in England, NIKKEI in Japan. We have to remember that, yes, an index is a great benchmark and tool to compare our performance, but, again, not all indexes are created equally.

Public vs. Private

When you see reports on the stock market and see those tickers in Times Square, know that these represent activity in public companies. There's a difference between buying public companies and buying private companies.

Trading in public companies offers you the protection of our system of laws and regulations. When companies "go public," they agree to provide all information about the business so investors can make informed decisions. An Initial Public Offering (IPO) is the first time they will offer shares of the company. You can be an owner of the company through the public exchanges. Public companies have to register with the SEC (the Securities and Exchange Commission). Registering is a big deal, because it gives you, a potential investor, critical information about the business. Public companies are required to submit all kinds of financial statements and disclosures.

After a company goes public, the advantage you have of owning shares in the company is your ability to buy and sell it on the secondary market. It's usually easy to sell your shares on the secondary market, which means you have easy access to your money (liquidity).

Public companies must regularly report on the business. Any information about their earnings or management changes—anything that can affect the stock price—the company is required to make available to the public. It's all about disclosure.

Private companies can also offer their shares for sale, but it's through a private deal that doesn't come with all of the protections we just mentioned. People will often make the rounds to churches and clubs soliciting you to buy into or invest in their private companies. You have to be very, very careful.

A private placement is different than owning shares of a publicly traded company. Shares of private companies are only offered to small groups, not to the general public. They do not register with the SEC. The disclosure standards are much lower, and there is no good secondary market. Once you buy those shares, most of the time you're stuck. That means they're very illiquid. We always say: Be very cynical when approached by one of these folks to invest, because you're taking great risk. And in a private placement, you have to sign paperwork saying you understand what you're getting into and that you know something about investing.

When it comes to public versus private, we say: Buyer beware! That private placement has greater risk. It is very illiquid. You can get stuck. Yes, you COULD have a greater reward, but many times they can result in a total loss. So, don't depend on just anyone's assessment of a private company investment. Do your own homework. Be very cynical. Read all the paperwork. Understand what they're going to be doing with your money when you give it to them, and make an informed decision.

What is a Bond?

A bond is a debt obligation. When you buy a bond, you are loaning somebody money. If you buy a bond from the State of Mississippi, you're loaning Mississippi money. If you buy a treasury bill, you're loaning the U.S. government money. If you buy an IBM bond, you're loaning IBM money. Once you loan the money—that's the face—you get interest. In the U.S., you are paid interest every six months—again, typical bond. Then, when the bond matures, you get the face back. There are some variations to how this can work, but, generally, that's how bonds operate.

Treasuries

One of the safest places you can put your money is in a treasury. Treasuries are bonds. Remember, when you buy a bond, you're loaning money to someone. In the case of treasuries, you're loaning money to the US government. Since this type of investment is looked at as very safe, the tradeoff is in the return. With less risk, you expect to earn less return.

We have three main types of treasuries. We have T-Bills, which have maturities up to one year and can even mature in as little as three months. Then, we have treasury notes whose maturities are up to five years. Finally, treasury bonds have maturities anywhere from ten to thirty years. All of these are treasuries, all loaning the government money.

Although they're bonds, the T-Bills work a little bit differently in that the interest rate is built into the purchase. You buy them at a discount. So a $10,000 bond may only cost you $9,800, for instance, and when it matures you get the full $10,000 back. Treasury notes and bonds work a little bit differently in that you pay $10,000 (about) for one, you get interest twice a year, and at maturity, you get the full $10,000 back (if that's what you have loaned the government).

And the rates on these? Rates are low right now. CD (Certificate of Deposit) rates are not good. But we also remind people: We don't really have inflation (or not much inflation), so those numbers are real returns. Don't worry about those low rates if the investment suits your risk profile.

Treasuries are, relatively speaking, safer than CDs, and for that reason the rates for treasuries are lower. It doesn't entice too many people, but if you're looking for safety, that's where you might want to put your money.

To purchase treasuries, you can go through your local broker and trade them just like stocks, or you can go directly to the U.S. government through their Treasury Direct Program of the Federal Reserve Bank.

Unlike CDs, with treasuries you aren't penalized if you end up needing the money out. This is because treasuries are generally very marketable, meaning you can sell them to someone else. Even if the treasury hasn't matured yet, but you need your money or you want to invest in something else, you can sell it to another investor on the open market.

If the treasury is in a taxable account, you will pay taxes on the interest. You need to understand this is not the same as dividends and capital gains. It is interest, and it is taxed at your income tax bracket.

Portfolio

Your portfolio is your collection of investments. This can include stocks, bonds, real estate, gold... anything under the sun. Understand that a mutual fund or an ETF is similar to a portfolio. It may be a collection of only stocks or only bonds or only gold, or it could be a collection of everything altogether.

Diversification

Diversification is all about lowering your risk. When people think about diversification, they often think about combining different types of investments in a portfolio. Hopefully, you do this in such a way that you offset risk. You can also diversify by not putting all of your eggs in one basket. By this we mean using different banks or using different bank accounts so that you make the most of the FDIC limit of $250,000.

Some people even use different financial advisors. That's fine, but don't get too complicated. Imagine if something happened to you, and your family members had to find all of these different accounts. You also may be putting a limit on any of the discounts you could receive with your smaller accounts. Most advisors have breakpoints in the fee structure, meaning that the fee is tiered. Once certain amounts are invested with the firm, the fee on money over that limit is charged a lesser fee. Be mindful of your fees and of what services are provided. Remember, if you aren't sure exactly what the services are that the advisor provides to you, ask!

Regarding companies with stock share options, as long as you have a diversified set of investments within the 401(k) and some other investments outside of that, we think it's okay to invest in your company's stock. Understand that as long as you are working for the company, you're basically an insider. You need to be paying attention to things such as: What does the company look like? Are they giving raises? Are they giving bonuses? Are people happy working here? Or do you see a problem with your customers? Because as long as you feel good about the company and the prospects of that company, then it's okay to invest in the stock. Once you leave the company—and this is what happens to a lot of people, they change employers and they still have stock in that old company—well, now you're no longer working for them. You no longer have the inside track. At that time, it's often better to cash out and invest in something different. But as long as you're at the company and you're paying attention to the company's health and prospects, then it's generally okay to hold these positions.

You can also diversify to lower your taxes. The problem that we see with many people we work with is that by the time they retire, most of their money is in tax-deferred accounts: 401(k)s, Traditional IRAs, etc. In this type of situation, we consider a Roth IRA conversion. This involves moving that tax-deferred money into an account that is tax free. So, now if you need to purchase a car or take a big trip, then you don't have to worry about creating a big tax liability by withdrawing that chunk of money from a 401(k). Another thing to keep in mind: Those Roth IRAs have no required minimum distributions (RMDs), which means you have more flexibility on when and how to withdraw the money.

How do you do a Roth conversion? There is no income limit, so anyone can do a Roth conversion. Work with your CPA, though, because you don't want to bump yourself up into a higher income tax bracket. You can also consider a partial conversion. If you leave the account alone for five years, you'll get the full benefit of tax free growth. It's wonderful. But, also know that if you have to, you can dip into the original amount you put in.

In terms of starting out with investments, the first place to turn is your 401(k). Then, if you have some extra money, you want to build a good savings account. You can also make use of a Roth IRA beyond your 401(k) depending on your income limits.

Liquidity

Liquidity is all about how fast you can convert an asset to cash—real cash. Liquidity is relative. An emergency cash fund—a good savings account or a money market account—is very liquid. It's more liquid than your house. Your house is an investment, but it's not a very liquid investment. You usually can't quickly turn your house into cash. Bonds take a little bit longer than your money market. Stocks a little bit longer. And as you go up into real estate, that can take a while. It may take six months to a year to sell a house or a piece of property.

With all of your investments, you have to consider how liquid you need to be. We caution against putting all of your cash into something that's pretty illiquid like real estate. You still need to have some cash and some near cash to get your hands on in case of an emergency.

What is an Annuity?

Annuities are insurance products. We have two main types of annuities: fixed and variable.

Fixed means that your rate is fixed, usually once a year or once every few years. They invest typically in bonds.

A variable annuity works like a 401(k). In other words, you have investment options or mutual funds within the plan. You choose the funds you want to invest in, and whatever those funds earn, that's what you earn.

We're starting to hear about a lot of these annuities popping back up, because companies are putting riders (extra layers) on these insurance-type products. These extra layers can cost you a lot more money.

The reason people are enticed into putting money in annuities? Well, if you go down to your bank and you're looking to invest in CDs, the rates are very low. When you start to hear of any product offering a little bit more, you start chasing that yield. People are also enticed because these products are usually marketed as having "guaranteed returns," which makes them sound risk-free. People hear "guarantee" and neglect to read the fine print. And, trust us, there is a LOT of fine print to read. We would warn you: Don't be enticed by that guarantee. There are all kinds of little stipulations to it. Be very cautious. Read everything, and if you don't understand what you're reading, take it to an independent third party to help you understand the contract. We find that most people really don't fit the profile for an annuity. If you do want to put some money in, don't put everything in there. Limit how much you put in, because it is very inflexible.

Annuities have very high annual costs. Your basic annuity is going to be 1.8% to 2% just for the basic annuity. That's to start you off. Then, you're going to have extra fees that come on top of that. They also have limited investment choices, which means if you use a variable annuity, you have to use THEIR choices. And the biggest problem with annuities are the surrender charges. It makes them very inflexible, because you can't get to your money. Typical surrender charges run six to nine years with very hefty penalties if you want to withdraw money before the surrender period is over. If you have something that happens (and, of course, with six to nine years, anything could happen) and you need that money, you are faced with paying a steep penalty to get it.

As far as riders are concerned, we liken them to extras. It's like going through the line at Piccadilly, and you get the basic entrée with two vegetables; but if you want dessert, it's extra. And your tea is extra. That's the way these riders work. You start with a basic annuity (1.8%). There's one that's become very popular; it's guaranteed interest. The typical guarantee is around 5%, but people think that's guaranteed on the balance. It's really guaranteed as to your monthly income sometime in the future. The average cost of that guarantee is 1%. So you're getting a guarantee of 5%, but you're paying 1% for it. Figure that one out. You can also have guaranteed death benefits. Because these are insurance products, they like to stick that one in. The cost of that is about an extra 1%. So if you get those two, plus your typical annuity, now you're paying almost 4% for this product when you can find other investments out there that cost you less.

One more thing: There's a great article by Lisa Gibbs that talks about annuities called "No Pot of Gold." We would encourage you to read that before you sign on the dotted line.

What Should You Expect From Your Portfolio?

Investing in stocks is a long-term game, and you have to expect volatility, meaning fluctuations in the market. With stock market investing, volatility just comes with the territory. Stocks do offer the best opportunity for growth, though, and that's why we invest. Just don't be surprised when they bounce around. Remember that we define a market correction as a 10% decline. Understand that sometimes this happens very quickly, but more often than not, it's a gradual step down. You only realize you've hit that 10% mark when you're there.

We have a hero in the investment business, John Bogle, who says: Don't do something; just stand there. Sometimes when you get into these market corrections, this volatility, the best thing you can do is to sit tight. You need to understand the difference between a correction and a change in the business cycle, meaning we might be having a recession.

If there is a recession (declining growth), it takes longer for the market to get back. But if it's just a change in investor perception, then often that downturn is short-term. Investor perception can be affected by anything under the sun.

What's the best way to protect yourself against volatility and roller coasting in the market? The first step is to have a good strategy. That means your asset allocation. What are you invested in in the market (stocks vs. bonds vs. real estate)? Have a well-diversified portfolio—not all your eggs in one basket. You're going to have investments that move at different paces and directions. Only change your strategy after the dust clears. When the market is in the midst of declines, it's not the time for you to go say that you don't want to be in stocks. But once the market settles, you can decide whether or not you're cut out to weather that kind of volatility and consider adjusting somewhat.

Working With a Financial Professional

What to Bring to a Meeting

Working with a new advisor can be daunting. In the first meeting, both parties have a lot to learn about each other. The advisor should make information about themselves and their abilities available to you through a website or mailing before the meeting. What they learn about you, however, depends entirely on what you decide to tell them.

What you need to bring will depend partly on what you hope to accomplish, but in general, the more information you give your advisor, the more specific and useful the advice you receive will be. Take the time to think about what you need to bring and gather the following important items.

- Your spouse. While both partners do not need to earn the same amount, or even participate equally in household finances, it is very important that you and your spouse understand how the other thinks about money.

- Account for all of your assets. Ideally, you will have statements for bank accounts, investment accounts and retirement accounts. In addition, know the value of your home and any other significant property you own.

- Tally up your debts. The important information about debt is the balance, interest rate and payment terms. At a minimum, write down the balance, interest rate, monthly payment and expected maturity date. Make sure to include everything you owe: credit cards, student loans, car loans and mortgages.

- Know your income and how reliable it is. Bring a pay stub if you have one that shows your gross pay and any withholdings. If you work a regular job, this is easy. If you work on a freelance, part time or contract basis, you'll have to do a little more work estimating what your income will be in the future.

- Know your specific goals. If you plan on buying a vehicle, home or college education in the near future, write down how much you expect that to cost.

- A notebook. Your advisor should send you a record of any actual recommendations they make for you. You should still take notes and have somewhere to keep your questions written down.

- Your story. Your advisor needs to work with you, and to do that they need to understand who you are in order to tailor their advice to you. Be prepared to talk about how you view the money you have and what you want it to do for you. While you don't have to bring in every transaction statement, a clear idea of where your money goes each month is critical. In addition to these standard things, your unique situation and goals may demand more specific information.

- Tax returns. If you have complicated taxes, are meeting with a CPA or are looking for ways to lower your taxes, bring a tax return. It will be useful for your advisor to see if you've missed any good deductions.

- Real estate information. If you are looking to buy a new home or move, bring information about what your new home might cost. Details about the area will be useful in helping determine what you can afford and how much your lifestyle and finances will be impacted by the move.

- Children or parents. If you are helping manage your parent's affairs, or looking to pass on wealth to your children, ask ahead of time if you should bring them. An advisor can help you determine what is appropriate information to share and provide factual information for the relationship.

Remember that an advisor cannot help you with things that they do not know about. The more information an advisor works with, the better your advice will be.

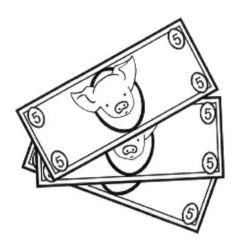

Plan for the end of the world.

Investing for the End of the World

If you are preparing for the end of the world, you might be buying gold, guns, canned food and remote property in the foothills of the Rocky Mountains. After all, you will need to be self-reliant for food, shelter, water and defense. Hone your large scale gardening skills now, because the canned goods will run out eventually.

The Fear Trades

When the market gets weird (read: goes down sharply, or at least 10%) there are a few investments people tend to reach for: Gold and long term US Treasuries are two of them; the Swiss Franc is sometimes another one. US Treasuries are generally viewed as a risk free asset. They are bonds, so you can easily calculate the value and the cash flows; and they are backed by the US Government, which is generally believed to be a reliable credit. After all, why would the US Government default when they could just print more money to pay the bond?

Of course, there are risks with that US Treasury bond: if the government does just need to print money to pay obligations, inflation will likely erode the value of the dollars you will receive. To understand this relationship, think of supply and demand. If there are more dollars being printed to chase roughly the same amount of goods and services in the economy, each dollar will be worth less in comparison to the goods or service it is buying. Another risk is interest rate risk. If interest rates rise after you buy the bond, the market value of the bond will decline. After all, why would someone pay the $100 that a 3% yield cost you if they can go out in the market and buy a 4% yield for the same price? This is a bigger risk with longer term treasuries. If you are planning on holding the bond until maturity, this does not much matter, but it can look bad on your account statements in the meantime.

Gold and Swiss Francs are both viewed as stable money. Historically, gold was a unit of money, and until recently, the value of our dollar was actually measured in gold. As long as nothing too exciting is happening in the world, gold typically tracks inflation. This means that it preserves its real world value—this is why it is considered a "real" asset. Since it preserves its value in the real world, if you fear imminent collapse of your nation, economy and currency system, it might be a nice way to hedge that fear. Investors typically either love or hate gold. "Gold Bugs" as they are known like that gold will be there for them even during rampant inflation or societal collapse while the haters just think it's a dumb shiny thing that doesn't do anything fun. It is possible that both sides are right.

Our main concern with gold as something to hold if the world collapses is that there is no guarantee that people will take your gold in exchange for necessities like food and drinking water. If they did take it, you would probably need plenty of small change in gold, and a scale for measuring your gold flakes and dust. Tricky stuff. There's also a practical tax consequence that gains on the sale of gold are taxed at a minimum tax rate of 28%—potentially higher than your marginal tax bracket, particularly if you lost your job as society and the economy crumbled. If you traded your gold for food or services, you have some flexibility in how you report the value, particularly in a situation where there is no ready market for the goods. However, faithful reporting of income and expenses is a cornerstone of our democracy (which may well be collapsed at this point), and transactions like this may invite a time consuming audit (time better spent out there growing your food, right?).

Swiss Francs are sometimes viewed as a safe haven trade in weird times, too. Switzerland is known for its policy of neutrality, excellent chocolate and building bunkers in the Alps. It can be easy to confuse the safety and homogeneity of the country for real world economic or financial security. Maybe you can hitchhike to Switzerland when the world ends. Maybe your local café will take Francs when you venture down from the Rockies for a morning pick-me-up after the Apocalypse. We're not totally sure about this one.

There is a breed of investor that is permanently bearish. They often sell stocks short on generalized worries or keep the fear trades going even when it isn't working. There is always a crisis just around the corner that they believe, to the contrary of the built up evidence, that humankind just won't make it through. These investors are the ultimate contrarians.

But HOW Will the World End?

The problem is that we don't know exactly how the world will end. Will it be a mild end, with stock markets functioning as staff moves computers to higher and higher floors as the oceans rise? Will it be all at once with an asteroid that we only saw a few months in advance? Will it sneak up behind us, cutting off one piece of our economy at a time, leaving us with only Twitter to speculate about what is actually going on?

Maybe the end of the world will be even less of an event than we anticipate. Maybe governments will fall peacefully, and after a few years of anarcho-libertarian communes someone will have the idea to build a highway to their cousin's commune, and we will come together to figure out how to pay for it, accidentally forming a government in the process.

However it ends, it may be on your to-do list to prepare for it. Let's explore what you can do with your investments.

If you believe that some environmental disaster will end the world, consider companies that are working to fight that end. Depending on how long this disaster takes to play out, your companies could have a string of profitable quarters as they try to clean up the mess we have made or stem the tide of rising waters. Ecology & Environment or Clean Harbors specialize in cleanup of disaster sites as well as providing environmentally sustainable solutions to polluting industries. Companies that make solar panels or operate wind farms may be of interest, too.

Maybe global conflict will be the downfall of man. In this case, we have plenty of defense related stocks that will benefit from military spending. Don't forget your personal safety. A company like Ruger or Smith and Wesson also outfit private individuals, mercenaries and militia right in your neighborhood!

The end of the world could come in a variety of ways. It is important that you take the time to think deeply about what you are most afraid of and position your investments to protect against those fears in an appropriate manner.

When The World Is Over, What Does Anything Mean?

It might strike you as prudent to avoid investing in stocks. After all, stock markets can close for a variety of reasons. After the terrorist attacks of September 11, 2001, American markets closed for four days. If the market is closed, you may have a hard time selling your stocks, so it's best to just avoid them, right? Not so fast! Your broker will still hold your stocks and may make valiant (or not so valiant) efforts to calculate their value and help you with trades. There is a robust over-the-counter network in the US, and we are not so old that we have forgotten how to use phones (getting there, though). Transfer agents will be there to help brokerages affect trades on your behalf. In fact, when the global stock markets shut down at the beginning of WWI, brokerages continued to trade and quote securities' prices, though clearly liquidity and price discovery were affected.

What if Your Brokerage Is Insolvent?

A general financial crisis might bring down a couple of brokerages, but if you keep a paper copy of your latest statements, you'll have a starting place if your brokerage disappears. SIPC insurance covers the first $500,000 of your cash and securities if your broker is insolvent. It's fairly common for larger brokerages to cover the next $49,500,000 of your account with private insurance. If you are concerned about this, you should take note of that insurer in case you need to file a claim. It is important to note that SIPC does not protect against fraud if you never actually held the securities or against the loss of value. They really just protect the custody function—the safekeeping and access to your securities.

If brokerage insolvency or exchange shutdown is the specific risk you are trying to protect against, try keeping your stocks all in paper certificate form. While a burglary is probably more likely to strike your home than an exchange outage, fear is not rational. We generally do not advise that people keep paper certificates. Not only are they more likely to get stolen, but they are much harder to trade and generally have much higher fee structures than an account at a discount broker. If worse comes to worse, however, you can trade your Mondelez shares hand to hand for packets of crackers and a bit of peanut butter. You would just need the certificates, though a notarized bill of sale might come in handy. If you're the one receiving the shares, check with the transfer agent to make sure that you are doing the transaction correctly, because you will want to ensure you receive the shares when the ledger opens back up (usually the first Monday after Judgment Day).

You might not want bonds either. Depending on the state of the legal system during and after the end of the world (let us not forget that the end of the world may be a prolonged, nine step process as outlined by Dante), companies may decide to default on their debt obligations, and bankruptcy proceedings in the afterlife could well favor equity owners if sufficient time has elapsed for you to make a claim on the assets of the company. This is a weird situation to be in, but the end of the world might have weird quirks.

An alternative to regular, registered bonds may be to look up some bearer bonds. Bearer bonds are bonds which neither the company nor any transfer agent or bank keeps a record of who the owner is. Interest is paid literally to whoever holds (bears) the bond. Generally, you clip off a coupon and mail it in for the interest (this is why interest payments on bonds are called coupons). You still have the risk that someone steals the bond, but at least they won't hack your account password. Bearer bonds are a little bit frowned upon these days, but they do still exist. If you find some from a company or government with excellent credit and good chances of surviving the Apocalypse, you may be able to get them at a good price in the turmoil. If people don't put a premium on tax evasion, yet haven't realized that the bonds are still money-good, you might get a good deal on them! Keep in mind you will have a small window between the realized Apocalypse and the next coupon payment, which will be a reminder to the owner that they still have something of value. Act fast to get the best deals. Try eBay.

So, securities are a mixed bag, and you can't trust your broker to hold GLD for you as you are raptured. How are you supposed to invest in the most fearful of investments—gold? We've already discussed the tax implications, but maybe you are counting on the IRS being out of commission as well. That is fortunate for you; just watch out for the marauding charms of magpies.

Practical Tips on How to Prepare for Huge Change

A few years ago, Ryder had the opportunity to hear from a fund manager about his vision of the end of the world. It was a combination of financial and societal collapse, peppered with cute anecdotes about him darning his socks on the flight over. It was all a bit surreal, looking back. In the event of huge shifts in society, government or economy, self-reliance was the most valuable thing. He was impressed that Ryder was an avid cyclist and gardener and a little taken aback that Ryder (at the time) had chickens in his backyard. We think this put Ryder in an elite tier of those who were truly ready for the worst.

He did give Ryder an interesting way of looking at crisis. His vision was one where inflation made financial transactions difficult; eroding trust and decaying infrastructure limited the use of online shopping and the use of credit. Self-reliance was indeed the investment to make.

Part of self-reliance is frugality—if you spend most of your time, money and effort eating out and paying other people to perform tasks around your home, you are ill-prepared for a time when those services aren't available. While you don't necessarily need to move to the foothills of the Rockies and stock your bunker with canned goods, learning to take care of a home you own and grow and prepare your own food has value in itself. Physical skills are not only useful in a pinch, but are imminently traceable in the current economy and possibly to the next economy.

A collapse of the financial and economic order does not mean that you need to have alternative methods of payment handy. Your bitcoins will do you little good if there is no electricity or internet. Instead, build your social capital and help others build theirs. Knowing people who have resources or skills you may need will be valuable. Don't just network to build your professional prospects—strengthen your useful social network, too. Befriend a handyman or an expert food preserver or someone who has had enough outdoor adventures that surviving while lost in the woods is second nature. In countries where persecution of individuals based on some belief is more common, strong social connections are useful when seeking refuge from a monstrous government. Where goods and services are hard to come by, tight-knit communities must provide for each other.

People often put an over-emphasis on real assets, but the choicest bit of land or the shiniest gold coin will not save you if there is no rule of law. Having useful skills and a community that you contribute to will serve you well when your house, or country, burns down.

We don't know what the end of the world will look like, and we haven't bothered to calculate how likely it is to end, but preparing for it by bettering yourself and others around you should pay dividends in the current economy anyway.

New Perspectives, Inc.
Financial Solutions
www.newper.com

Nancy Lottridge Anderson, Ph.D., CFA
Ryder Taff, CFA, CIPM
Susan E. McAdory, MBA